BUSINESS STORIES

BUSINESS STORIES

16 Inspiring stories of Successful MSME Enterprises from SURAT

ASLAM CHARANIA

Notion Press

Old No. 38, New No. 6
McNichols Road, Chetpet
Chennai - 600 031

First Published by Notion Press 2016
Copyright © Aslam Charania 2016
All Rights Reserved.

ISBN: 978-1-946048-52-3

This book has been published with all efforts taken to make the material error-free after the consent of the author. However, the author and the publisher do not assume and hereby disclaim any liability to any party for any loss, damage, or disruption caused by errors or omissions, whether such errors or omissions result from negligence, accident, or any other cause.

No part of this book may be used, reproduced in any manner whatsoever without written permission from the author, except in the case of brief quotations embodied in critical articles and reviews.

About the Author

Mr. Aslam Charania is a business trainer, coach and a mentor to several MSME entrepreneurs. He has been into this field for past 12 years and knows the issues and challenges of MSME's, which helps him connect effectively with existing and aspiring entrepreneurs. He has addressed more than 1 lakh entrepreneurs through his open seminars, have trained more than 2000 entrepreneurs through extensive short & long term training modules, delivered more than 350 public speeches and has worked with more than 60 enterprises as consultant or a coach. He is a serial entrepreneur himself and is currently the chairman and managing director of mastermind group of companies, which has created 3 enterprises and an NGO in past 6 years.

Aslam also has penned a book "Retail Mahayudh" along with 2 co-authors, published in 2007. The purpose of that book was to boost the confidence of small and medium sized retailers from unorganized sector and empower them with ideas and tools so that they can not only survive but achieve healthy growth in their respective businesses inspite of aggressive competition from modern trade and online retail.

Acknowledgements

As is true of any meaningful projects, this book too, could not have been completed single-handedly. Being a business trainer, consultant and a founding partner in four organizations, I was very busy and occupied with a number of projects. I could hardly manage to interview all the entrepreneurs and give a final shape to their stories all by myself. Therefore, this book is a reflection of the efforts put in by a lot of people.

However, this book is simply not all about compiling interviews and giving a final shape to it. It includes a lot of editing, content corrections, laisioning with the entrepreneurs for interviews, cover page design and many more such tasks.

It is because of the unconditional support and efforts of lot of people that I've been able to successfully complete this project.

First and foremost, I would like to convey my gratitude to all my teachers and my parents who have made me what I am. It is their teachings and efforts due to which I am able to do everything in my life.

Secondly, I'd like to express my gratitude to all the entrepreneurs whom I have interviewed and have covered their stories in this book. They have been kind to spare their time and share their experiences with me. They have been very candid and honest with me. It was fascinating to see how eager they were to share their story with other aspiring entrepreneurs through this book. Without their kindness, openness and generosity, this book would have not been possible.

The next in the list of acknowledgement is my entire team of mastermind who have provided me with unquestioned support and encouragement throughout the project. They had to accommodate my requirements and endure a lot of trouble on my accord. But, they have done it all with a smile. In fact, they have managed well even in my absence, although; they had to face lot of challenges. They are my core strength, they are my pride and they are the source of my happiness.

I would like to especially mention names of few of my team members who has made a remarkable contribution in this project. Rinki Singh and Mrugesh for laisioning and getting appointments with all the entrepreneurs. Rinki Singh again for managing the entire interview process with an equal passion for the project. Roshni for post writing support during the editing and finalization process and also for managing my schedule as my personal assistant and reminding me regularly about all my pending tasks through her persistent follow ups, she had ensured that I complete this book at the earliest. Yashaswini and Tanisha for correcting the book and giving it a good shape.

I also would like to mention that the inspiration to write this book has come from all our clients whom we have served for the last 12 years. It was while we were working with them that I realized that there is a need for cross learning for entrepreneurs. MSME enterprises are largely unorganized and they need a lot of encouragement and inspiration to change. Thus I decided to work on this project. I offer my deepest gratitude to all of them.

This project would not have been possible without the support of my publishers and the editors, I would like to thank them from the bottom of my heart.

Last but not the least I'd like to thank three very special women in my life, my wife Minaz, my lovely daughter Aarzoo and my mother Amina. During this project and also during my entire journey of the past 12 years, they have been the ones who has suffered a lot, they had to compromise and adjust a lot to my priorities and business requirements. Without the unconditional support from the family, one can't achieve great success. So is true in my case and I remain really grateful to them.

I thank you all from the bottom of my heart. Thank you for being there for me and for supporting me in this very meaningful work. Hope this book is able to make a difference in the lives of many.

Thank you

Author's Note

India today has emerged as a land of great opportunities. India is the youngest country of the world, we have 2nd largest consumer base, we are one of the fastest growing economy of the world. According to price waterhouse cooper reports on India that they published in august 2014, by 2030, India has potential to be the 3rd or the 5th largest economy of the world. We are biggest supplier of the human talent to the world. We have huge middle class with constantly rising per capita income. Such great opportunities were not available to us in past few centuries. It is our time to think big, do the right things and make it big.

In spite of such great opportunities, we don't have as many globally competitive enterprises and are struggling with unemployment, poverty and illiteracy, Why?

Based on my experience of more than 12 years as a business trainer and a consultant for several MSMSE organizations, I am convinced that entrepreneurs and entrepreneurship can be one of the effective response to these challenges and opportunities. Entrepreneurs create jobs, develop innovative solutions to address the need of the society, they increase GDP and thus attract lot of foreign investments and can help this nation in a significant way. It is an imperative for us to promote entrepreneurship.

Through this book I am trying to contribute my bit. It is completely based on real life entrepreneurial stories. The entrepreneurs themselves, through personal interview shared their stories with me.

It is my conviction that if we want to promote entrepreneurship in this country, and if we want the existing entrepreneurs to grow, we will have to first and foremost try to increase their confidence so that they take greater calculated risks and target rapid growth.

Author's Note

One of the best way to increase their confidence in the business, the economy and in their own future is by sharing the stories of other entrepreneurs and enterprises who have made it big in life, who have passed through rough patches and yet have managed to convert their micro startups into a strong enterprise.

The stories covered in this book are real life testimony for other entrepreneurs. Before succeeding, these entrepreneurs too had struggled, they too had faced threatening challenges, they too have faced tough competition, they too had started small, they too may not be that much qualified, they too are from small town, they too have faced legal and bureaucracy issues, they too had no one to support, they too had struggled for funding. Yet they made it big in life and have set the right example for all of us to learn from and get inspired from.

They have defied all odds and created their future out of nothing. They are the examples of what a passionate entrepreneur can create, if he/she has the will and determination to do.

This book has also been written to find the answers for the following questions that are always on my mind and I am sure that it might be the same with millions of entrepreneurs. There are millions of MSME enterprises in India but very few have made it really big and have created successful businesses. Very few have progressed from micro to small, from small to Medium & from medium to large companies.

- Why and how did they create such successful enterprises?
- What is it, that majority of the entrepreneurs fail to understand or implement?
- Why majority of the enterprises in India remain micro or small even after investing 20, 30 or 40 years of their life in business?

What is it that we all can learn from these stories and grow in our respective businesses is the core theme of this book.

This book is written especially for millions of entrepreneurs from MSME sector. I want them to read this book, learn from these business stories and implement those learning's to develop a strong business for themselves.

Author's Note

The second set of people whom I want them to read this book is the youngsters who are willing to start their own enterprise and make it big in life or the youngsters who will join their existing family business as 2nd or 3rd generation entrepreneurs. This book will prove to be one of the big resource for them. They can learn from others mistakes, their wisdom and also from their experience so that these youths can prepare well before launching their venture and also that they achieve faster growth.

Thus:

> *"Encouraging The MSME Entrepreneurs and Youths To Create Big, Sustainable Businesses And Generate Employment Through Their Work Is The Core Objective Of Writing This Book"*

This is just the first edition of my mission in which I am covering 16 business stories exclusively from Surat city. Later on, I would be working on business stories from Hyderabad, Mumbai, Ahmedabad, Rajkot, Pune etc. My actual plan is to cover stories from 50 leading cities of India.

10 Habits of Highly Successful Entrepreneurs

I am presently working on developing a training module for MSME entrepreneurs. Esp. for those who have high aspirations and ambitions in life but are unorganized and are struggling to actualize their true potential and fulfill their dreams.

After lot of observations and introspection over my last 12 years of experience, I have come to a conclusion that there are certain habits or characteristics that all the successful entrepreneur's possess and practice in their routine. These habits, if developed by other entrepreneurs, will enable them to achieve greater success. These habits can lead them to prosperity and growth in their personal and professional lives.

These are the same qualities and habits that you will find in most of the entrepreneurs and enterprises covered in this book. And also from as many entrepreneurs you might have read or known about.

Habit 1: They have clear vision and goals supported by effective planning

Habit 2: They re-invest their profits back into their business and allow it to grow big [they never drain profits from their business]

Habit 3: They take full advantage of all the available technologies to improve efficiency and create a competitive advantage

Habit 4: They believe in the power of marketing and branding and focus hard on it

Habit 5: They build strong and smart teams and delegate effectively

Habit 6: They focus hard on operational excellence to remain price competitive and are good at financial management

Habit 7: They network with better and bigger people

Habit 8: They convert their business into a force for good, do business with greater sense of responsibility and are keen on making meaningful contribution for the development of the society

Habit 9: They learn and explore a lot

Habit 10: They are very disciplined and live a well-balanced life

Almost all the business stories covered in this book demonstrate the above qualities in variable measures, but they have it. This is what differentiates them from others, this is what has helped them to grow and achieve considerable amount of success in their entrepreneurial journey. And this is exactly what I want all the other entrepreneurs to learn from this book.

Aslam Charania

Happy Reading

Please read only one story at a time.

If possible, Read **"TWICE"**

Please read between the lines:

They were asked about the;

Importance of Team

Importance of Technology

Importance of Family

Importance of Education &

Also about the Importance of constant learning for an 'Entrepreneur' to be successful

While you read, please try to understand the entrepreneur's Mindset, attitude and over all approach to business and Life. This will give you a fair idea about; why they could achieve, what they have achieved.

Stories sequence

1   SHREE RAMKRISHNA EXPORTS PVT. LTD.   3

Shri Govind Dholakia, in spite of belonging to a family of farmers, had his eyes set for a brighter future. And, what can possibly be brighter than the shine of diamonds. It is this pursuit that brought him to Surat from a small village of Saurashtra, at a tender age of 13. After getting the hands-on training while working at a diamond polishing enterprise for a substantial period, he started his own firm, which today is a renowned name in the diamond industry with an annual turnover of over 6000 crores INR.

2   NJ INDIA INVEST PVT. LTD   17

They started out as college friends but for Neeraj Choksi and Jignesh Desai, a simple friendship was never enough. They fostered a joint dream of making it big and thus this friendship developed into a partnership for greatness. They started their own Mutual Fund Advisory Services and currently have huge clientele base of 17 lakhs investors, dealing in 25000 crores INR worth of assets.

3   LAXMIPATI SAREES   33

Having to hold the mantle of the business at the tender age of 14, it was never an easy way up for Mr. Sanjay Sarawagi. From battling with his father's sickness to initial losses, he has braved it all. From the humble beginning, to managing a diverse yet extremely successful brand of sarees and ethnic garments, his journey has been an inspirational tale.

4   AALIDHRA   53

It all started out as a repair workshop and currently stands as a pioneer in the textile machine manufacturing industry. Gondalia family has led this company to the zenith of success, following the footsteps of its founder

Mr. Hansraj Gondalia. Today, Aalidhra is a name synonymous to supreme quality Indian machines and is an ever expanding venture.

5 MAGICRETE   67

For Mr. Sourabh Bansal, a huge order of a particular client at his family owned lime and other chemical processing plant, changed his worldview. He revolutionized the construction industry by initiating the production of AAC blocks, the latest technology in the construction industry. With the passionate efforts of an IIT graduate, Mr. Sourabh, his brother Siddharth [IIT, IIM Lucknow] and Puneet [partner's son] Magicrete is able to boost the business to about 150 crores INR of annual turnover. This is a story of dream, hard work and professionalism.

6 HINDVA   85

Migrating from a small village of Saurashtra, loaded with big dreams, Pravinbhai Kheni and Manjibhai Patel started working as labor in a diamond-polishing unit at Surat. Later in life they started their own diamond polishing unit M. Kantilal Exports and scaled it to popularity within no time. Today their business group 'Hindva' is a diverse conglomerate having ventures in the real estate, mines, textiles, diamonds, hospitality and health care having gross revenue of 1450 crore INR per annum. Hindva is currently one of the well-known names in construction industry.

7 F-STUDIO   97

Born to a family of zamindars, Mr. Subhash Dhawan a patriotic and passionate entrepreneur, always had the entrepreneurial zeal in him. He refused to be tied down to his father's textile retail stores and initiated a bolder step into the business world. His creation, Gokul Tex Fab Pvt. Ltd. & Retail Brand for natural fabrics 'F-studio' are currently, one of the popular names in the textile and the natural fabric industry, skirting a turnover of over 250 crores INR.

8 DHARMANANDAN DIAMONDS   107

As the second generation entrepreneurs, Mr. Hitesh Patel & his cousin brother's major challenge was to upgrade the initiative taken by their founders from first generation & modernize their business to make it contemporary. From introducing latest technology, to including bank funding in the process of production, they gave the business a new leash of life. Today, Dharmanandan Diamonds has an annual turnover of 5000 crores INR and is all set for further expansion.

9 PRAFFUL SAREES — 119

For Mr. Narayan Agarwal, the decision to run the business came at the cost of compromising on his studies. Yet, he took it up gladly and has brought phenomenal success to the brand 'Prafful Sarees'. their host of other businesses of embroidery, dyeing and printing, manufacturing of nylon yarn, retail etc. has enabled them to secure turnovers as huge as 550 crores INR. With the entry of 2nd generation, this group is all set to take a next big leap.

10 SAHAJANAND TECHNOLOGIES PVT. LTD — 131

Mr. Dhirajlal Kotadia had established the firm from an extremely modest background. From a seller of miscellaneous goods on trains, he founded the company as a provider of technological solutions to textile and diamond industry. His son Mr. Bhargav Kotadia's involvement in the business has brought in greater R&D initiatives and it's commercialization and thus Shahajanand group has grown into the predominant producer of heart stents, laser machines for diamond cutting and polishing, Ayurvedic medicines etc. housing the turnover of nearly 200 crores INR.

11 SOSYO — 151

Mr. Abbas Hajoori had to grapple with the threats from multinational giants like Coke and Pepsi and carve out their own niche in the market. As a second generation entrepreneur the responsibility of carrying forward the brand 'SOSYO' and its business successfully was a rather tough one. However, not only did he excelled in all such expectations but also ushered a 100 crores INR turnover for the company, thus securing its brand value in the market.

12 BHATIA MOBILES — 165

In the digital gadgets retailing industry of the western part of India, Bhatia Mobiles is a widely renowned name. But it was Mr. Sanjeev Bhatia's powerful vision and determination that led him to this stature, despite all odds. He transformed a simple STD PCO venture into a brand that is the leading retailer of digital gadgets. They have recently launched their own brand of cell phones 'HSL' and are all set to revolutionize the domestic cell phone market.

13 SUGAR 'N' SPICE   179

A self-made man, Mr. Sandeep Dawer created a food chain, whose fame and business has spread to every nook and corner of Gujarat and other parts of the country. Instead of following his father's footsteps as a doctor, he chose to start his own multi-cuisine food chain that has become the favorite eating out destination in several parts of India.

14 LUTHRA GROUP   193

For Mr. Girish Luthra, the challenge was to overcome the sharp drop in revenues in their business and transform their line of production into a more sustainable pattern. On the personal front, he had foregone his engineering degree to hold reins to the business but he consistently tried to acquire knowledge in the entire span of his career. Today, he not only is invited to the reputed institutions including IIM's for speeches but also is at the apex of a highly successful and popular textile and environment solution companies, 'LUTHRA' & 'GEPIL'

15 INDIAN WOMEN FASHION   213

Mr. Sunil Jain always dreamt about a life of achievement and prosperity and it was simply his perseverance that helped him realize this dream and made him the claimant to an over 100 crores INR turnover saree brand, 'INDIAN WOMEN' despite his humble roots. His enterprising nature and keenness to keep up with the changing times, have been the major contributor to his success.

16 ZOTA HEALTHCARE PVT. LTD   227

From a small retail drugstore into a pharmaceutical giant that has nearly 100 crores INR turnover annually, Zota has been a story of gradual growth. Zota family has spurred such progress by relying on upgraded marketing strategies, persistent scaling of the business and widening the product basket. It's a story of how a small retailer can scale and create a successful company, if they have passion to grow and dreams to fulfill.

DIAMONDS THAT SHINE ON THE SOCIETY

Shri Govind Dholakia

Chairman

Firm Name:

Shree Ramkrishna Exports Pvt. Ltd.

Estd: 1970

Products or Services:

Polishing, Trading And Exports Of Diamonds And Diamond Jewelry

Shri Govind Dholakia, in spite of belonging to a family of farmers, had his eyes set for a brighter future. And, what can possibly be brighter than the shine of diamonds. It is this pursuit that brought him to Surat from a small village of Saurashtra, at a tender age of 13. After getting the hands-on training while working at a diamond polishing enterprise for a substantial period, he started his own firm, which today is a renowned name in the diamond industry with an annual turnover of over 6000 crores INR.

Shree Ramkrishna Exports Pvt. Ltd.

"I have never compromised on my values and principles till date. Even today I live with same values, principles, thoughts and humility as I used to stay in my village Dudhala when I had nothing."

... Shri. Govind Dholakia

I was born in a joint family in Nov. 1947, the year of our independence. We are 5 brothers and 2 sisters and I was the fifth child. The total strength of joint family was 40 which comprised 17 brothers and 13 sisters all staying together under one roof.

To sustain a huge family, both; my mother and father had to work in fields for the entire day to meet the ends. They took lot of pain to raise us. I studied till 4th standard in our village Dudhala and further studied till standard 7th in nearby village Lathi.

We had heard a lot about Surat's diamond polishing business and the scope of employment in this industry and thus On 2nd April 1964 at the tender age, I came to Surat for the first time along with my 2 elder brothers, started learning the ghat [bruiting] work in one of the local units and stayed with 23 people in one small room. My first salary was Rs.103/- and it came after 6 months. It was a very good amount for us in those days.

After couple of years in Surat, due to recession, I had to go back to my village and even had to work in farms for some time. I came back once the market got better.

"Business has been a great teacher, it has taught me lot of things about leadership, management, entrepreneurship and global economy."

Starting our own business:

It was in 1970 while I was working in unit of Laljibhai Kheni along with my couple of friends, Bhagwanbhai Patel and Virjibhai Godhani that we thought of establishing our own diamond-polishing unit. And on 12th of March 1970 we started our business with small amount of Rs. 5000/-

My first international tour to Antwerp, Belgium was in 1977 with the help of my godfathers Shri Shantibhai Mehta and Shri Navinbhai Mehta from D. Navinchandra & Company. This tour exposed me to the outside world, I saw the tremendous potential that this business had. It expanded my horizon and vision and that lead us to rapid growth of our business.

Once I started growing and learning about the available opportunities, I gradually started inviting all my brothers and cousins one by one to Surat and settled them all. Today each one of them is well settled and happy and looking at this, I am the happiest among all.

Business has been a great teacher, it has taught me lot of things about leadership, management, entrepreneurship and global economy.

The business was running good and was growing rapidly, but in 1983 one of our partner Shri Virji Godhani was diagnosed with cancer and could not survive. At that point of time his both the children were small so we continued Virjibhai's partnership till his children grow up. In 1995, we all 3 partners decided to split the partnership and move ahead on our own. Virjibhai's sons started Godhani Gems, Bhagwanbhai Patel started Bhargavi Gems and I managed SRK. I am very happy that today, our families and we all partners are well settled.

❝ *We believe 'Problem is progress'* ❞

Expansion:

In 2004, realizing the huge market potential, we launched our jewellery manufacturing and trading unit as part of 'forward integration', under the name of Jewel Goldi India and later we started S Goldi. Today we have a very strong foothold in jewellery markets of New York, Mumbai and Hong Kong.

We believe 'Problem Is Progress', and the next point will explain this belief. One of the major turning point for us came in the year 2008 during global recession; there was a huge crisis in diamond world, many people left this business, several others reduced their workforce, several decided to reduce their production, and some of them decided to temporarily shut down.

While majority of them were reducing their workforce, we sustained all of them; which helped us greatly during the revival phase. We took the advantage of the scenario and maintained the steady operations and production. When market started accelerating slowly and demand started to grow, nobody had on-hand stock, especially of fancy diamonds, but we had. This helped us to gain good business, decent profits and above all we won the trust of the market and our team. This helped us to grow faster. We are growing at 25% and above each year since then.

In 2011, we realized that demand for fancy shape diamonds was increasing drastically all over the world. Observing this change, we strategically decided to reduce our production of regular round shape diamonds to 50% and devoted that production capacity to produce fancy shape diamonds and this worked very well for us.

We also have online selling platform through which we connect to all leading buyers across the world and we participate in almost all leading trade shows globally.

> *❛❛ I wanted our 2ⁿᵈ generation to be well prepared for future responsibilities. I wanted them to face the harsh realities of life before they step into our shoes. ❜❜*

Current Status:

Today Shri Ramkrishna Exports [SRK] is among the top 3 diamond processors of India and one of the leading firm globally. Our turnover in last financial year was 6000 crores and we are having the team of more than 7000 people in our workforce.

We have our offices in 6 countries which includes cities like Antwerp, New York, Telaviv, Hong Kong, Dubai and Shanghai. We sell diamonds to more than 175 countries.

Our current head quarter building is India's first energy efficient construction created with the help of magnetic chiller technology.

Considering the huge labor crunch in this industry, we have established our own institute 'Shree Ramakrishna Export Research and Knowledge Center of Diamond' that prepares the skilled workforce as per our need.

Policies that lead us to success:

We believe in 'up through the rank' policy and never hire any outsider in senior position. We promote only the internal members to senior positions and train each one of them to fit into their roles.

Normally the 2ⁿᵈ generation enters the business once they are young or after the completion of their studies. They immediately acquire top positions as part of their entitlement as the son or relative of the leader. Mostly they are unprepared and might have not experienced the harsh days of struggle like their parents have. I did not want to commit the same mistake and wanted our 2ⁿᵈ generation to be very well prepared for future responsibilities. I wanted them to face the realities of life before they step into our shoes. Thus contradictory to the tradition, I sent my son Shreyans and his cousins to different cities after their graduation

> **For me discipline, patience, self-control, honesty and spirituality are important and I wanted our children to practice all this before taking up the charge of this company.**

without any money or support and asked them to survive there on their own.

They worked in the hotel, washed dishes, did all types of work to sustain themselves and in the process they learnt many important lessons of life, which they could not have learnt from any institution of the world. They learnt about the hardships of life, they learnt about the value of money and above all they learnt the lessons on humanity. And these are the very important learnings, which I thought they should have before they join our family business.

For me discipline, patience, self-control, honesty and spirituality are important and I wanted our children to practice all this before taking up the charge of this company.

I have never compromised on my values and principles till date. Even today I live with same values, principles, thoughts and humility as I used to stay in my village dudhala when I had nothing.

Our Belief System:

Life has taught me many lessons and those lessons and experiences have shaped our beliefs. We run this business and manage our personal lives, based on this set of beliefs. They are practiced at all levels in our organization.

Few of them are:

'I am nothing but I can do anything'; all key members of our organizations frequently repeat this statement. This reminds all of us about our own power and potential and also makes us belief that impossible is nothing

Next belief is *'Sampatti ane santatti prabdh thi male, tena mate prayatno ni jarur chhe, paap karvani jarur nathi.'* [you will get wealth and prosperity as per your destiny, and for that, all you have to do is put right efforts. But

❝ people is progress ❞

you don't have to cheat]. This reminds everyone that we should never take short cuts or cheat anyone for any kind of benefits. If you put right efforts with honesty, your destiny will definitely change.

Four words that I have applied in my life are; 'Chalse, Bhavse, Favse Ane Gamse'. Which means; I don't need special treatment, everything is ok with me. I can adjust in any situation. Thus, I am comfortable in every condition and situation. I can manage with whatever I have and would not complain about anything. These words remove complexities from our lives and make it simple.

Fourth is *'People is Progress'*; I love my village dudhala and always crave to stay there but if there is no work force, how can my business grow? So if you don't have people, you can't grow. Always build teams and take excellent care of them. If they are with you, you will definitely win.

Make people yours, care for them because when people start loving us, they start giving their best and thus we grow.

Our Work Culture:

Apart from these beliefs, we follow certain routine in our organization. Our day starts with prayers and ends with positive energy and satisfaction. We treat all our team members as we treat our own family, take great care of their needs, ensure that they are happy in both; their professional as well as their personal lives. We solve their personal problems too. At times we also get involved in fixing up their marriages.

We have provided them with the best possible facilities for sports, physical fitness; we provide them healthy and hygienic lunch. We play with them, we dance and we celebrate with them. In Diwali we try to share our profits generously and give them attractive bonus.

This does not mean that we compromise on any of the organizational discipline. In fact, we are very strict in some of our policies such as 'vyasan

> **❝** *I always tell this to people when I address: "if you don't accept technology proactively in advance, before others, once five to ten key players in your industry accepts and uses it, you will be forced to use it for your survival, but that will not give you the necessary competitive advantage* **❞**

chhodo athva company chhodo' [leave tobacco and other addiction or leave the company]

There was a big depression in 1979-80 and we could not earn anything is the entire year. Even at that point of time, we maintained the team and infrastructure. As a result in Aug-Sept, when there was a sudden rise in demand, we earned more than previous year's annual profits because we had stocks. Opportunity can be encashed only by people who are ready.

That recession was so intense that 2 to 3 banks in Israel which were dependent on diamond industry, closed down. The rates of diamond dropped by 80%. We have survived such phases and have emerged stronger, because of our effective policies and beliefs. People who have not seen such depression have not tasted real depression. Today's depression is nothing; instead, today's market is much better.

Use of modern technology:

Technology has played a crucial role in our progress and growth. Since 1962, we have changed or upgraded our technology for more than 20 times. Right from 1970 to the galaxy planners that were launched last year, we have always adopted latest technologies proactively.

I always tell to people when I address them: "if you don't accept technology proactively in advance, before others, once five to ten key players in your industry accept and use it, you will be forced to use it for your survival, but that will not give you the necessary competitive advantage". The choice is yours, be proactive and be a leader or be reactive and be the mere survivor.

Initially when Sarin planner was developed in Israel, they kept the technology for themselves and did not share with rest of the world. After 2 years, they decided to launch it worldwide and kept it for display at Antwerp. We bought couple of machines and tried, got decent

> **❝ 'While investing in latest technology or any new ideas, don't look at the cost but look at the ROI as a parameter' ❞**

benefits, so we ordered 5 more. One of my friend who was the dealer for Sarin, asked me about the benefits of Sarin, I gave a general reply that benefits are good but the machine is very expensive [25 lakh rupees per machine]

He said let us analyze the benefits, we took diamonds of various size and processed it with and without Sarin [the difference was 6%] and once we calculated the benefits, we realized that these machines can be free in just 4 months [the ROI was great] – that day I learnt an important lesson, that 'while investing in latest technology or any new ideas don't look at the cost but look at the ROI as a parameter'.

Upon this realization, we ordered 100 Sarins upfront, investing 25 crore rupees. Very few people thought like us and had guts to invest heavily in latest technologies.

After a year all adopted this technology, but we got one full year and in that year we made wonderful profits, developed excellent competitive advantage and covered big market. Technology alone is not enough. Combination of great technology & well trained manpower to operate that technology creates wonders.

My Values and Principles:

I am a follower of Dongreji Maharaj, he has taught me that always think about happiness of all, even for your people. If you think about their happiness, you will be happy yourself. All you need is generosity.

We are very generous with our people and ensure their growth and prosperity. As a result, even with tight rules, they have stayed with us for decades.

He also taught that "don't try to change people or improve them, just improve yourself. If each person improves itself, the world will improve"

> ❝ *Govind kaka is a leader of SRK, he is not SRK. – Organization and I are different and I have to play an effective role and justify my role as a good leader* ❞

We should not keep ourselves on high pedestal. He taught me that this world is a theater and you are given a role. A role can be of owner, of a labour, of father, of husband or of brother. I am given the role as a boss; I have to perform excellently in that role. In different contexts, I have to play different roles. In office 'boss' and at home 'husband'. We play approx. 50 different roles in a day.

Govind kaka is not SRK. SRK is a set of ideology, system and a set of principles and values.

Govind kaka is a leader of SRK, he is not SRK. Organization and I are different and I have to play an effective role and justify my role as a good leader and my workers have to justify their role as a workers. Once we all are out of SRK premise, we all are humans and are equal. We should treat all with equal respect and take care of each other. This has been our philosophy and core focus.

We take care for education of children of our team members, we take care of their accidental needs, and even get involved into fixing their marriages. Ultimately all should be happy. We are connected with their families, our relationship with them is of 24 hours.

Social contribution:

Shri Govindbhai Dholakia is a servant leader in a true sense. Not only did he took great care of his team members and their families, but also is one of the leading contributor of Gujarat for all types of social developmental activities.

Through the six family owned trusts and as a trustee of more than thirty other trusts, he has contributed in abundance for education, medical and health facilities, disaster relief, environment protection, water resource management, city development etc.

He believes that *"To develop the society, first educate the society"* ['Samaj ne viksit karvo hoi to pehle tene sikshit karo']

> **My main motto behind starting this award is to associate the name of my mother with the great personalities whose name and work is going to be remembered for centuries and thus the name of my mother will also stay in the memories till centuries**

He also runs a relief center at Katargam area of Surat where he visits daily for 2 hours and listens to the grievances and problems of citizens personally and helps them with money, guidance and any other support they need.

More than 3000 students receive scholarship from his efforts and is also a leading donor for several hospitals and trusts. He has developed several schools and hospitals, developed few villages, also adopted 2 villages at Kutchh, post 2001 devastating earthquake and rebuilt them.

He is also the member of Saurashtra Jaldahara Trust that has created more than 125 check dams in the Saurashtra region of Gujarat. There was huge water crunch, which forced people to leave Saurashtra and it also affected the income of farmers. Today due to this trust and the efforts of these trustees, Saurashtra is full of water and the agro production as well as employment has grown substantially.

He has started an award in the name of his mother "Matushri Santokben Dholakia Manav Ratna Award" and this award is given to outstanding contributors and achievers who have done something meaningful for the development of the larger society. Started in 2007, till date this award is given to the great people like Shri Dalai Lama, Shri Vargese Kurian, Shree APJ Abdul Kalam etc.

I loved my mother a lot and no one in this world can take her place and match with her greatness and thus I started this award in her memory. My main motto behind starting this award is to associate the name of my mother with the great personalities whose name and work is going to be remembered for centuries and thus the name of my mother will also stay in the memories till centuries.

For his exceptional contribution, he is being awarded by Surat Municipal Corporation with 'Suryapur Ratna Award'. Awarded by the southern Gujarat chamber of commerce and industry with 'Best Citizen Award'. By GJEPC in 2001 as 'highest diamond exporter of India'

> ❝ I must have read life of at least 50 successful people. I don't read novels or imaginary writings. I am not interested in imagination of others, I am interested in reality, and I want to read about real life experience. ❞

He has also been invited to speak at various trade groups & institutions including IIM Ahmedabad as a guest speaker. IIM is also planning to introduce SRK case study as a study material. He is also invited to speak and share his knowledge in various institutions, communities and organizations of India and other parts of the world as well.

He is also involved with several organizations that work for the upliftment of diamond industry and its future.

When asked "how many people benefit from your social activities?" he replied, "I don't know, some efforts produce zero result and impacts no one. And at times, a small advice impacts hundreds of people"

We just have created a system and framework for social contribution, we have developed institutions and put it on auto mode, so that it moves on and can impact multiple generations.

Counting benefits is not my job, my role is to just do the good work.

Practicing what you learn is important

I heard Dongreji Maharaj 25 years back, and I still remember most of the statements i heard several years back. Because I put it into practice immediately.

At the age of 14 years, I had Bhagwad Geeta by heart. Once I heard Bhagwad katha and got a divine experience and that inspired me to read Geeta – the social aspect developed since then.

I must have read life of at least 50 successful people. I don't read novels or imaginary writings. I am not interested in imagination of others, I am interested in reality, and I want to read about real life experience.

Prarabdh [Destiny] and Purusharth [Efforts and Hard work] both are like 2 wheels of a bicycle. If one is not working, the bicycle will not go ahead. thus I did both. I did lot of hard work and best efforts and left the result to destiny. People say that you can't get more than your destiny

> ❝ *As of now world diamond market is of 1 lakh crore and we are doing approx. 6000 crores [6%]. Our first target is to reach 15%. Until then I don't think we need to diversify or look for any other business* ❞

but the fact is that destiny also is developed only through hard work and effective efforts.

Future Plans:

We are not looking for major diversification in near future. As of now world diamond market is of 1 lakh crore and we are doing approx. 6000 crores [6%]. Our first target is to reach 15%. Until then I don't think we need to diversify or look for any other business. Focus is very important in life and in business.

Although we have invested approx. 500 crores in solar technology, software and in jewelry manufacturing as our forward integration strategy. This all is for the satisfaction of our future generation, which is growing.

To my children, I don't give any advice, I just share my knowledge and wisdom with them. That too, when asked by them or when they face some problem, and leave it up to them whether to implement it or not.

Advice to other entrepreneurs:

- If you want to be happy, change your nature and behavior. Be honest and ethical. Unethical person may grow overnight but will have great fall in relatively short time.
- Whatever business you want to do, learn it thoroughly at least for 1000 days. Start only after you have got necessary practical experience.
- There is no shortcut to success. Be hardworking, truthful and honest.
- Select the field as per your interest, don't do anything for the sake of money. And never take unnecessary debt and over burden yourself and your business.

POWERED BY SIMPLICITY AND FOCUS

Mr. Neeraj Choksi & Mr. Jignesh Desai
Chairman & Jt. MD

Firm Name:
NJ India Invest Pvt. Ltd.

Estd: 1994

Products or Services:
Mutual Fund Advisory & Investment Solutions

They started out as college friends but for Neeraj Choksi and Jignesh Desai, a simple friendship was never enough. They fostered a joint dream of making it big and thus this friendship developed into a partnership for greatness. They started their own Mutual Fund Advisory Services and currently have huge clientele base of 17 lakhs investors, dealing in 25000 crores INR worth of assets.

NJ India Invest Pvt. Ltd.

'We always wanted to make it big in life'

.... Neeraj

This is the story of Neeraj and Jignesh, two college friends who revolutionalised the investment sector with their innovations.

We met at vidyanagar while studying and were sharing the same room. Jignesh has engineering background & I have management, said Mr. Neeraj.

Since our college days, we had thought to start something in financial service sector, as it required minimum capital to start with. We always wanted to make it big in life.

I had an opportunity to work at Baroda stock exchange for six months and saw ring based trading. thus we started with stock trading services from nanavat, Surat. This is how we ventured into the business world. Our company name was NJ capita stocks. We started NJ India Invest Pvt. Ltd. In 1994.

To start with a professional approach, we brought a computer and a software program from capital market. It was a gutsy decision because the computers were expensive, but it was necessary. I was always focused on research and constant research required a proper infrastructure.

It was a physical market and had huge risk of bad delivery on the broker, we have experienced almost all of them.

> **❝** We both were clear that we don't want to focus only on earnings of today, rather we will always look for better options and also take considerable amount of risk, if that leads to a better future. **❞**

Mutual Fund Focus:

1994 was the year when mutual fund industry was opened up for Pvt. Sector, prior to that only public sector companies were allowed. This was a new opportunity for us. We did a full fledge research on mutual funds and its different aspects and realized that it is much better option for investors.

We instantly decided to exit from stock broking and focus on mutual funds. In a way we risked the existing income. It was another bold step for us, but we both were clear that we don't want to focus only on earnings of today, rather we will always look for better options and also take considerable amount of risk, if that leads to a better future.

We decided to lose few thousands to make it big. We were also willing to have couple of bad years, if required. From that day we started eating, drinking and thinking about mutual funds. This was 1996.

It was not a blind risk. We studied a lot about the different companies in this sector and attended lot of seminars, we made sure that the decision we took was very well researched and well calculated.

Doing what you feel right is imp. And have guts to focus only on it. In those early days of liberalization, all the other financial service providers were focusing on Fixed Deposit's, Insurance and Stock Broking but we chose a different path and had a single-minded focus.

From 1997 our focus on mutual funds increased a lot. When market penetration of mutual funds was less than 1% of total investment or savings market. If you have a passion, everything will fall in place.

This decision of exclusively focusing on mutual funds market had its own challenges. We were early entrants in the sector so had to educate customers about it, but we also had early entry advantage. Converting non-user into users was a tough task, especially due to lost trust of investors on mutual funds due to Harshad Mehta bubble burst. MF investors lost lot of money during that crash.

> *Between 1998 and 2003 the growth of NJ as well as the MF industry was good and we got decent success. But then came a major change in the commission structure of mutual funds, which forced lot of players to go out of business.*

Mutual Funds industry was in itself in the process of change. Pre-1992 phase, UTI was the monopoly. Unit 64 was giving some assured NAV, which was not right or was against the basic principles of MF market.

Later Morgan Stanley entered the market and they said we will take only Rs. 300 crores as AUM [asset under management] but they received a very healthy response from the market with proposals for 1000 crore. After proper consideration finally they accepted 1000 crore.

Between 1998 and 2003 the growth of NJ as well as the MF industry was good and we got decent success. But then came a major change in the commission structure of mutual funds, which forced lot of players to go out of business. Earlier the customer had to pay 2% entry fee on MF investments and that 2% went to agents and brokers as their commission. Later SEBI abolished that entry load and our margins eroded.

While others left, we persisted because of several reasons. Since we had closed all our other services and focused only on MF's, we had too much at stake and had no options to move away. Secondly, we also realized that MF's was very much beneficial to the investors and it will only increase their confidence and investments into these products. Thirdly, we used better technologies to eliminate inefficiencies and reduced our cost of operations.

We applied lot of innovative ideas and somehow managed to survive, while others left. It is similar to product trading where as DSA or distributor or agent or as a retailer; you find that suddenly your margins are reduced. We faced the similar challenge. The trader's response to it would be reducing cost and improving scale – we did the same.

Current Status:

Today we are operating in 19 states, have 99 offices, 1400 employees, 21000 advisors, 17 lakh customers and 25,000 crore asset under advice

> **NJ Group is a leading player in the Indian financial services industry known for its' strong distribution capabilities.**

[AUA]. Approx. 10 lakh people invest with us regularly every month. Each month, we invest Rs. 300 crores through SIP in equity market.

Our annual revenue is more than 300 crores from NJ India Invest. Other businesses are also generating minor profit share.

NJ Group is a leading player in the Indian financial services industry known for its' strong distribution capabilities. NJ Wealth Distributor Network, earlier known as the NJ Fundz Network, started in 2003 is among the largest networks of financial products distributor in India.

We also have our insurance service wing 'NJ insurance', which we launched 4 years back. In insurance we focus mainly on pure risk products related to health, auto & life. Our insurance business is growing at 50% premium amount each year and considering the fact that India is the youngest country of the world and majority of youths are uninsured, we have a great potential to scale.

We also have an education company NJ Gurukul. We are associated as training providers with FPCP [CFP training], they are present in more than 50 countries. We train and prepare advisor for financial services industry and also recruit some of them as our advisors.

Apart from FPCP, we also run MPHI training module, which is compulsory for people advising or dealing in mutual funds. As IRDA is compulsory for insurance advisors, MPHI is for MF's advisors. Each year we train 30,000 people at multiple locations.

We are also associated with AAF [American Association for Financial management] for programs on estate managers and wealth management.

We have a real estate arm, which currently is focused on Dahej, Gujarat, a very upcoming territory. We have completed 3 projects so far. One of them is the first row house project that has received green certification from World Bank.

> **"** Our success is mainly due to our efficient operations and use of all possible advance technologies in each aspects of our business **"**

Earlier we used to sell properties developed by other developers but it did not match with our value system. We could not assure deliverables to the customers and were not able to give clear delivery time and that is what we don't like, so we decided to exit from distribution. Now we develop our own projects.

NJ technologies is an IT company which delivers software solutions. Team of 400 people is working in it. Initially the company was started for supporting our own business and 99% consumption was in-house, but now, we are looking forward to provide software solutions to asset management companies from both; domestic as well as international markets

We have a holding company in Mauritius, 'NJ Global Invest' which provides advisory platform and financial products distribution support to entities from global markets and also guides domestic retail investors on global investments. It has a back office at Dubai.

Key success factors:

Our success is mainly due to our efficient operations and use of all possible advance technologies in each aspects of our business. The other factor is our support system and care for all our channel partners and investors.

We call all our branch office as partner service centers and all advisors as our partners.

Market fluctuations are high and NAV rates are volatile so we have provided an online platform to all, loaded with all possible analytical tools so that they can run the business with great agility and efficiency. Our partners can see their business trends with all the possible analysis and check their profitability, and their clients can visit on this platform and view all their investment details with all possible analysis.

We also have developed and shared 'Bizmall' with them, it is an online application loaded with all the necessary stationary designs

> **In a way we are creating new entrepreneurs and providing them the handholding support through our technological and other learning tools.**

and ready newsletters, which they can customize, print and deliver to their customers using their brand name. Even the newsletters when it is supplied, it carry's our partners brand name. This helps them grow and create a strong brand. We also give ideas on how to get clients and promote themselves, how to generate leads, how to convert clients, etc.

Apart from this online platform, we also provide them lot of free and paid trainings for their advancements and progress. Their success is our business now.

If an individual can create customers, we can give them every resources and infrastructural facilities so that they can do good business and grow effectively.

In a way we are creating new entrepreneurs and providing them the handholding support through our technological and other learning tools.

We could grow exponentially because we made right choices. We always had a choice to do everything ourselves or grow exponentially by creating a smart organization that develops the network of thousands of advisors, We opted for the later.

We recruit advisors and train them. Provide technological and operational support and help them in marketing, promotion, CRM, etc.

To select the right and committed advisors we used to charge 1500 rupees' registration fees to register with us. Those who don't pay this amount are not committed players was a clear demarcation.

No one in our industry used to charge any fees. It was all free, even with the much bigger organizations. But we had a very strong belief in ourselves.

There is one practice that we have followed since day one and that is; we pay all our advisors on a fixed committed date every month. Even if we have not received our commissions from the companies we work

> **Three sectors that drives the GDP of India are: financial services, infrastructural development and IT. We have sharp focus on all three**

with, Whereas others have the practice of paying only after they receive the transfer from parent companies.

Once you have systems, process and policy in place, things automatically go ahead. But along with this, you need a good quality team and effective channel partners for strong distribution, market reach and effective execution.

Our principles and standards were very clear and transparent, that has helped us a lot.

Focus on few ideas is must:

Market offers lot of Complexity in products – to remain simple is difficult in this complex era. But somehow we have managed to remain simple and focused. This is why we have not faced much challenges.

We have kept our product portfolio simple. We have focused on MF's, SIP's, Insurance etc. We never got into commodity trading or derivative or foreign currency and other products for making quick money for ourselves or for our customers too.

Three sectors that drives the GDP of India are: financial services, infrastructural development and IT. We have sharp focus on all three effectively and have diversified in those businesses to maintain the good portfolio.

We have never tried to diversify in non-core areas and have maintained a good focus, that is why our growth has been great.

Our core values:

Our values and principles are also very clearly understood and strongly practiced:
- We never sell the products which we ourselves won't like to buy
- We prefer to offer only those products which are genuinely good for customers

> **While markets have grown 7 times in past 10 years, we have grown 30 times.**

That is the reason why we stopped selling real estate products because we found that developers are not delivering as per commitment. They failed on all three parameters; quality, amenities and delivery deadlines.

If customer losses a single rupee due to our mistake, we don't discuss, we straight away cut the cheque on the customer's name without any further discussion. This our teams also know; thus they don't even ask us in such matters.

As a result of all the above steps, while markets have grown 7 times in past 10 years, we have grown 30 times. 10 years back we used to have total AUA of 300 crores but today it is 25000 crores and our gross income is 300 crores.

Challenges Faced:

Each business has its own challenges, we too have. When markets drop, it is very hard to maintain the energy of investors, advisors and our team. That is the major challenge.

Our business is linked with the market, and the market is very volatile & outside our control. To maintain the trust of our customers and encourage them to invest regularly is the constant challenge. It's a never ending story. But all these years of experience have helped us to learn how to deal with challenges and thus, they don't seem like a threat.

Doing business is exciting:

We believe that through our business we deliver certain benefits to all the stakeholders and this is the most satisfying aspect of our entrepreneurial journey.

We make people rich with min. risk, we help them to save for long term and we help them be disciplined financially. Our avg. investors ticket size is Rs. 2000 or Rs. 2500 per month in SIP. [if they invest 10,000 per month for 30 years? @ 8% rate of return the amount will be 1.5 crore, @15% the amount goes up to 8 crores, @20% the amount goes to 23 crores].

> *We spend lot of money on staff training and upgrade them regularly. That is why we also have grown too fast and have been able to give them senior positions and promotion faster.*

If they don't invest their money, they waste.

While doing all this, we create employment for the society and the country. And above all provide growth opportunities to all our team members for promotion and income growth.

Role of team in success:

Our team has played a huge role in our success and they are the key stake holders in the entire eco system. With them; the relationship has been truly reciprocal. While we have provided them a good and respectable platform to perform, they have done lot of hard work to ensure growth of themselves as well as of this organization.

We have provided an entrepreneurial kind of environment under well-defined framework and systems and they have truly excelled.

Lot of people who joined us at initial stage are rich today and are at key senior positions. We have grown together and whatever we are, we are because of their contribution.

We spend lot of money on staff training and upgrade them regularly. That is why we also have grown too fast and have been able to give them senior positions and promotion faster.

For future growth, focus on 'customers'

Looking towards the future we have certain thoughts and plans on which we would like to develop our organization further.

Our mission focus would remain the same: 'Helping investor create wealth'

We have no targets in terms of numbers, the numbers will happen and the size of organization can grow up to 10 or 20 times automatically, if we focus on increasing the customer base and their investment size. Thus, we don't have to worry about numbers.

> **❝** We had very few products, few ideas, few principles and values. but sustained effectively for years and that is our key success factor **❞**

Our people should grow, our customers should grow, the numbers will automatically grow. We don't need to worry about them.

If we do the right things, the result will follow. Whatever we do, it should be in the interest of our customers.

We don't want to diversify or shift our focus; financial market, IT and infrastructure development has tremendous scope and there is absolutely no need to go elsewhere.

We have huge growth potential in our real estate business. At Dahej, 425 sq. km. land is being acquired by the govt. of Gujarat. If we compare it with Singapore, the total size of Singapore as a country is 515 sq. km, This is huge. Dahej has no housing facilities so we are focusing on developing housing clusters. Once housing happens, the market and other commercial developments, schools, hospitals, etc. will automatically happen.

Focus and discipline is must:

The ideas and good thoughts click to everyone but the key with us is that we have consistently sustained it since inception. We don't try twenty ideas for progress, rather; we have very few ideas but they are implemented with consistency and are sustained for long term.

We had very few products, few ideas, few principles and values. but sustained effectively for years and that is our key success factor.

Social Contribution:

We are equally committed to social contribution and run our own trust, which mainly works for education – esp. quality of education. We have observed that there are lots of dropouts after 7th or 8th grades, esp. from poor families. We have adopted some 100 students from this segment and are providing free tuitions to them at in-house developed classrooms. Our focus is to provide them quality education. We will hold them till their graduation.

> **"** At Kokery village (Gujarat), there is a person who has dedicated his life for education of adivasi kids; we are supporting him in his cause. **"**

We are not here for squandering money in the name of charity or getting some popularity, rather we want to ensure qualitative, tangible results. And for that we have developed certain system that helps us in achieving our objectives.

We took exam of some 2500 students, checked their reports, took 360* feedback from our expert panel and selected 100 students for our cause. We want to do it professionally and with best possible quality

To further scale this initiative and to reach out to the masses, we use technology to provide online education.

At Kokery village (Gujarat), there is a person who has dedicated his life for education of adivasi kids; we are supporting him in his cause.

We are active member of chamber of commerce. jignesh is vice president of Navsari management association, I am a member of rotary club of Udhna, Surat. With rotary, we work for skill development of dropout youths, esp. computer training, because everything is becoming digital and computer training will help them to get job on digital platform. This will empower them and help them do better jobs instead of laborious jobs.

Family's contribution in our success

Mr. Jignesh: Our success is due to constant support from several group of people. It is due to our team, it is due to our customers, our channel partners and above all it is due to the excellent support from our family members.

He mentioned that; Parents ensured min. burden on me so that I can focus on business development. Post marriage my spouse is very much aligned with our core objective and thus I get unconditional support. They respect what we do and all our activities, that is a great contribution. I am fortunate to have such wonderful family.

Mr. Neeraj: Mentions our parents had 100% trust on us, even when we were struggling. They never asked us or questioned us with doubts. Our wives have been very lucky for us, after their entry in our lives, we grew exponentially

> **❝** Role clarity between both of us is superb and well defined; we discuss only on strategic issues and avoid discussion on execution side. **❞**

We travelled a lot and were extremely busy, they were always there and managed all social aspects so that we can be free to do business.

Our partnership is our major strength:

It's been 21 years and we are still together, as strong as ever. Because our objectives are one and we both are aligned to it.

Our core is clear: nothing at the cost of the customer and our team should get better facilities and support from us.

Both partner's family go for joint holidays and we are like a one family.

Most of the time what we both think is more or less the same, In rare case, if it is not so? we understand that; you have to be accommodative at times and be understanding.

Role clarity between both of us is superb and well defined; we discuss only on strategic issues and avoid discussion on execution side.

Jignesh manages real estate and I manage some aspects of IT and the financial services mentions Mr. Neeraj

Problem starts when one of us starts thinking that whatever has happened is because of me. We are clear that in different situation any one of us can be right and in some cases, we both are wrong and some of our team members may be right. In such case we respect the team members view and accept whatever is right.

Constant learning is must:

Jignesh: I learn from everywhere. I learn from Narayan murthi and also from a kirana trader, as far as they are honest and ethical, they both are an inspiration for me.

Neeraj: I like people who are ethical and value based. I get inspiration from them. Popularity of a person to learn from is not at all important. If you are a billionaire but unethical, you can't be a role model.

> *Education develops the society and civilizes it. It builds your character. The process itself is enriching. It is a character building activity.*

Their views on importance of education:

Education plays a very vital role in human life and it is esp. important for an entrepreneur. One has to learn the technical aspects of their respective faculty with greater details and develop in-depth insights.

Education Is important and very critical. Apart from learning technical aspects of it, you also learn about your responsibilities as a human and as an individual, you learn lot of moral values, you learn to respect your teachers and other humans, you learn about your history and values.

I am glad that Right to Education is launched. Education develops the society and civilizes it. It builds your character. The process itself is enriching. It is a character building activity.

Advice to other entrepreneurs and aspiring youths:

- Always look for your customer's interest and the progress will come
- Be patient: you can't succeed without investing your time and energy for sustainable period.
- Don't start business or work just to change or avoid your boss.
- Don't think 'mujhe kya mil raha hai – think mai kya de sakta hu'
- Be generous with your team. Don't be greedy, think about their prosperity
- Be professional and ethical – pay your taxes. It is your moral obligation – to us no officer can ask for bribe because we have nothing to hide. And that is why our 100% energy is focused on growth instead of protecting self from govt. officers.

TORCHBEARER OF SURAT'S TEXTILE INDUSTRY

Mr. Sanjay Govind Sarawagi
Director

Firm Name:

Laxmipati Sarees & Dress Materials

Estd: 1984

Products or Services

Mfg. of Sarees and Dress Materials

Having to hold the mantle of the business at the tender age of 14, it was never an easy way up for Mr. Sanjay Sarawagi. From battling with his father's sickness to initial losses, he has braved it all. From the humble beginning, to managing a diverse yet extremely successful brand of sarees and ethnic garments, his journey has been an inspirational tale.

Laxmipati Sarees

"Since childhood I used to observe how my uncle and father were dealing with customers and were managing their business and learnt basic principle of selling and customer service. We used to serve water and tea to our customers while our seniors were dealing. That knowledge is helping us even today".

……… *Sanjay Sarawgi*

We belonged to a middle class family and before we shifted to Surat, my Father was into the trading business of suiting & shirting with other family members in a small town at Rajasthan

I was sent to convent school but could not cope with it and went to local school at Gorkhi, Gwalior.

Since childhood I used to observe how my uncle and father were dealing with customers and were managing their business and learnt basic principle of selling and customer service. We used to serve water and tea to our customers while our seniors were dealing. That knowledge is helping us even today.

Our business was started by my father, Shri Govind Prasad Sarawagi in around 1983-84. He started with weaving looms but due to reservation andolan – there was violence everywhere and our looms were burnt. The business was closed due to heavy losses.

> **❝** While I was 14, my father was severely sick for 3 years and I had to manage the business in his absence till he recovers. I was not a businessman, but a business boy when I entered into business. **❞**

In 1985, my father once again collected all the courage and started saree trading business. Financially, we were zero but my father had very strong reputation in market due to his sound policies regarding payments. He was very honest and professional in his dealings with others.

Because of his goodwill in market, few Surti Gujarati people trusted us, they not only gave us material and gray cloth but they also gave us money to restart. We are indebted to them, had they not supported us at the right time, we might have not been where we are today. "Hume mushkil waqt me Apno se zyada parayo ka support bahot raha" [in tough times, more than relatives, we got good support from others]

While I was 14, my father was severely sick for 3 years and I had to manage the business in his absence till he recovers. I was not a businessman, but a business boy when I entered into business. Our customers used to smile at us and were not taking us seriously.

We were competing against the big players in the industry. Even our suppliers were not sure about whether we will make timely payments or not. Customers were doubtful about whether we will deliver goods on time and with right quality or not. But with right efforts, hard work and right policies we somehow managed to survive.

After 1990, once we completed 5 years in business and understood the nitty-gritties of trade and we were also grown up, we started our expansion and went to bigger premise at JJ market.

My younger brother who was 2nd year drop out joined the business sacrificing his studies because I needed a helping hand once business scaled.

Our initial target was to sell 50 sarees a day to remove our expenses, but once we started and came in touch with people who were doing big business, we observed and analyzed their business practices to know

> **We have grown at avg. 20% CAGR in last 10 years and our market penetration is deep. Wherever sarees are sold in India, our products are available at each of those places.**

why they are so successful. Studying them had helped us and as a result, we achieved healthy growth. Currently we are well ahead of those industry leaders too.

Current status:

We have grown at avg. 20% CAGR in last 10 years and our market penetration is deep. Wherever sarees are sold in India, our products are available at each of those places. We export our finished products to several countries and now we also are targeting the fabric market for garments industry.

Today we are processing 1.5 lakh meters' cloth per day and have a target to process 4 lakh meter per day, by 2020.

Approx. 2500 people are working with us & last year our turnover in textile was Rs. 402 crores.

We are now entering into the manufacturing of salwar suits and lehangas. Also are in talks with couple of quality fabric weaving companies for international as well as domestic JV's, to produce fabric targeted for Europe market. Another reason for these JV's is to produce eco-friendly fabrics.

Recently we have collaborated with Dupont [USA] for corn based fabric - they will make fabric and we will be their processing partners.

"Samay badal raha hai, aur hame bhi hamari products me badlav lana zaroori hai." [time is changing and it is an imperative for us to change our product basket]

We are very aggressive with our future plans because we have all types of opportunities available for domestic growth and equally good potential in international markets due to rising demand of our fabrics and products. Apart from this we constantly focus on creating new fabrics, processes and products with the strong support of our R&D team.

> **❝** we freely share our ideas with other players from within the industry and also govt. agencies. We do this because we genuinely want the entire eco system to improve. We want people around us to come out of their traditional mindset **❞**

Our key success factors:

The major success factor for us has been;

1. Constant market research and R&D
2. Automization.

It is because of these factors that organizations like DUPONT came to us. We did not search for them, rather they got our reference from international market and they approached us.

We have eco-tex certificate and we are the only company from this industry, which has this certificate in entire Southeast Asia.

Our processing is also patented. It is only 8 years since we are into dyeing, printing and processing. But in all these years we have never followed others or accepted the traditional standards of working. Rather we have done lot of innovation and R&D and have developed a process that is very unique and eco-friendly, for which we have obtained a patent.

We have not kept all this knowledge and ideas only with us. Rather, we freely share our ideas with other players from within the industry and also govt. agencies. We do this because we genuinely want the entire eco system to improve. We want people around us to come out of their traditional mindset and trade practices.

Our work culture and policies:

Our current manufacturing unit is at Pandesara, Surat. We operate from 45 sq. yard property. Except weaving we have entire value chain in-house and this has helped us create meaningful employment for the society.

I believe we can contribute a lot through small but meaningful initiatives taken in our business itself. We prefer to first employ people who belong to BPL families, we have in-house hospital where doctors visit

> ❝ Jab Kaam hi unhe karna hai, toh behtar hai decisions bhi wahi le. *[If they have to do all the work and produce results? it's better that they take decisions]* ❞

twice a day for 3 hours each, workers get food for just 7 rs. per day [200 Rs. Per month].

For health, we provide free medication, health checkup camps and women related health awareness programs. Their surgeries or other treatment is free.

To support their kids in education, we provide books and other expenses [excluding the school fees] from the company budget.

We have full-fledged in-house facility for skill training. We train the freshers on skills related to retailing, languages and other soft skills. Fresher's who come from villages, we train them and place them with our wholesalers and retailers pan India. Till date we have trained and placed more than 1000 people.

To sustain this cause for longer duration, we have a simple process; the old and experienced people train the new comers. Once the new gains practical experience for few years, they become trainers and train the next generation.

Our principle has always been that 'Never break the commitments. Once made, fulfill it at any cost'. Treat everyone as your family member, even to your workers. We have people working with us for last 25 years and they don't want to leave.

We have trained them, trusted them, developed their confidence, delegated the responsibilities and also have given them decision-making authority and as a result, they are managing the whole business. We are just like trustees of this business. In last 20 years we have neither seen our stores opening or closing. Keys are with people.

'Jab Kaam hi unhe karna hai, toh behtar hai decisions bhi wahi le'. [If they have to do all the work and produce results, it's better that they take decisions]

Team plays the critical role in the growth of any business and I am one of the luckiest person in terms of having a great team. The team's

> ❝ *we don't sell our products, we send our products'* [Hum maal bechte nahi, bhejte hai]. *The day we have to forcefully sell, we will shut down our business* ❞

capabilities are developed to an extent where for any problem, some or the other person from the team has solution and thus, they don't bother me. As a result, we are free for new developments and market study.

Sales growth strategies:

For the growth of any business, customer relationship is very critical. The way we take care of our people, we take similar care of all our dealers and channel partners. Our dealers are working with us for 25 years and there is waiting of 5 years of people desiring to work with us.

We have always been different in our approach than most of the players from our industry, in whatever we did. This applies to marketing and sales management too.

To increase our sales, we have applied lot of new thoughts and ideas and went far ahead of others in terms of sales. We were the first one to develop a counter boy system in the industry. We were the first one to go for shop – in – shop [SIS] model. The dealers were reluctant to implement these new ideas in those days, but our persistence forced them to implement it. Today this is the most successful idea for sales growth and the entire market is following this pattern.

Later we started deploying sales boys at retail counters who exclusively focused on selling our products to end-users. This was something beyond the imagination of the entire industry. Even today, hardly few players use this idea.

We were among the first ones to launch catalogue system in textile products of Surat. The product was same but the presentation was changed. It created a very different impression and attracted lot of sales. This idea clicked so well with the industry that largely everyone has adopted it.

Our attitude is that 'we don't sell our products, we send our products' [*Hum maal bechte nahi, bhejte hai*]. The day we have to forcefully sell, we will shut down our business.

> **"We were selected as power brand in 2012-13"**

The customization in the presentations will help you get better sales. If the catalogue is for Dubai, I have to use international model and theme that relates with their aspirations and culture.

We are the only one that does not offer any schemes or promotional offers for sales. We don't spend money in Bollywood style branding and high-end marketing activities, my creation and ideas bring sales for me. Instead, we invest more in technologies for reaching the next level. The cost at which this publicity comes, is very expensive.

We were selected as power brand in 2012-13.

Innovation in production:

The differentiation we brought in our product creation was; we sourced copy right designs from international designers and exhibitions from several countries and also have internal design team that helps us in creating excellent designs. Designs are not Indian or international, design is just a design and it depends how you use it.

I was the first person from Surat to buy rights for designs from Paris.

At first they treated us like untouchables because the perceptions about Indians was that they will come to see the designs and copy it locally, they will not buy.

The people were shocked to see an Indian company buying designs. We did It regularly and bought designs in good numbers. In the process we developed a good reputation for Indians over there. We were hot customers for them. While others were purchasing 2 or 3 designs from them, we purchase 50 or more designs at a time (each design costs 400 euros)

This business has a lot of visual appeal to it. In men's wear you have plain, stripes or checks in shirting fabric. But in female wear the designs, taste, color, trends and new varieties are critical for success.

> **If we calculate the total cost of all our current machines, it will be approx. 200 crores. We do this because all advance technology saves lot of electricity, water, coal, gas, time and above all human labor.**

Use of modern technology is critical in manufacturing:

Technology is a blessing for us and for the society. Technology toh bhagwan hai, aatma hai, oxygen hai hamare liye aur sabhi businesses ke liye *[Technology is god, it is soul, it is like an oxygen for us and for all the manufacturers]*

"Nokia aur iPhone ka farq aapko istemal karke pata chalta hai. Agar aap personal use ke liye technology and costly gadgets me invest kar rahe ho toh phir apne business ke liye ya manufacturing me kyo nahi?" [if you spend a lot on personal use latest gadgets, then why can't you invest in latest technologies in your manufacturing?]

Today I am able to strike high value deals with someone in Lahore while sitting in Surat, without even having to meet him personally, all this is possible because of using new technologies.

We have always made huge investments in technology. If we calculate the total cost of all our current machines, it will be approx. 200 crores. We do this because all advance technology saves lot of electricity, water, coal, gas, time and above all human labor. As a result, in spite of investing heavily in technology, we are price competitive. "Aap bail gadi se ja rahe ho toh kitna waqt lagta hai, rail gadi se kitna aur plane se kitna? Technology hamare liye plane ke kaam karti hai"

Our technology costs us three times more than conventional machines. Yet we are price competitive and we have much better quality. Which helps us to rule the market.

We save lot of water and air pollution in the entire production process. i.e. for washing of fabric post dyeing and printing, people use kundi where constant water flow is required. Approx. 2 lakh liter water washes 38000-meter cloth in 24 hours. Whereas Korea has developed washing machines in which, for washing 70,000 meters of cloth it requires only

90,000 liters of water. If we use those machines, our investment will be free in just 2.5 months. And the best part is that you save lot of water, which can be used for other meaningful purpose.

We have air dyeing in which we use only 1% water compared to the traditional dyeing process. Per kg cloth in conventional dying takes 10 liters of water, we need only 100 ml.

We are wasting water in large quantity and damaging the society & civilians. Approx 1.5 lakh liters of water is wasted per machine per day. Each mill can save 8 lakh liters of water per day and we have 500 such mills, can you imagine the amount of water that can be saved?

Our Government recognizes the need and thus provides lot of subsidies on applied capital and on interest cost in various manufacturing sectors including textiles. We need to take advantage of these facilities and upgrade our technologies.

Instead the traditional thoughts are not changing, due to which large majority of traders of this market are not upgrading with the time and as per the market demands. It is because of which, people like us are growing faster.

Ignorance and traditional thinking is damaging the entrepreneurs, their businesses and the society as well. Instead of blaming the government for everything, if each one of us tries to improve ourselves, collectively we all will produce better results.

"Zyadatar log hume kehte hai ki tumhi aisi machine dal sakte ho, toh bhai hum hi dal sakte hai, aur kya" [A lot of people tell us that only you can invest in such technology, and we say, so be it]

We are way ahead of our competitors:

No one is our competitor and we don't consider anybody as our competitor. Every new innovation in surat textile processing business has been initiated

> **" Bail gadi aur rail gadi me competition possible hai kya "**

by us, so there really isn't anybody to compete with. [*Pehle hamari tarah banao toh sahi, hamare level ki technology toh install kijiye phir hamari competition kijiye. Hamare level ka kaam kijiye, hamare level ki quality deliver kijiye, hamare level ki designs toh banaiye. Main kis se compete karu, sab kuch naya develop humne kiya hai. Aur aaj aisa koi kar nahi raha*]

We have Japanese, Italian, German technologies and machines, we have license for international design usage, we have developed new fabrics, new methods of doing business.

"Let them first develop at least 50% of our technologies to be eligible to compete with us. A cart can never match up to a rail engine." ["Bail gadi aur rail gadi me competition possible hai kya"]

This is not my arrogance, but a harsh reality. People are not ready for today. I want to challenge them; I want to encourage them to change.

Key mistakes:

Just like other entrepreneurs, we too have made certain mistakes, which I would like to share. Few years back, we created the best process house as per industry standards and invested heavily into expensive technologies but we made a hiring mistake and as a result we went two years behind. The person was the master of old technology and we made him head of new technology and worst part was that the appointed person was not willing to learn about the new technology. The goods produced in that period had high goods return ratio. Approx. 50 lakhs meters of fabric came back as a goods return [GR].

This resulted in heavy financial loss, but we accepted the fact, corrected ourselves and created better product with greater care. This mistake increased our awareness and focus on quality and proved as a blessing in disguise.

> **Mindset and beliefs play an important role in an entrepreneur's life.**

Future plans:

From where we are today, we see huge scope in textiles and the future is bright. Our vision is to achieve 2500 to 3000 crore turnover in next 10 years. The road map and the blue print for it is already prepared.

Why most Businesses don't grow?

Surat has a good reputation in international market, but our traders and manufacturers are not ready to deal with them. There are buyers ready but manufacturers are not.

The same opportunities are available to all but our traditional weavers and processing houses are operating on job work model and are not producing their own products and also don't do much R&D. As a result, most of them are operating with survival mindset. We blame market but not ourselves. It is we who are not changing with the time.

Mindset and beliefs play an important role in an entrepreneur's life.

Most of the time people are crying and complaining that the markets are not good and that their businesses are facing recession. But this is not true. All can grow and almost all the players have equal opportunity to scale.

People fail to run a profitable business even after getting land at Rs 1 per gaj, whereas we made profit despite paying Rs 5000 per gaj. (sq. yard)

Their intentions are not right. They always focus on getting extra discount and on how to reduce electricity bill amount. Their major focus area is saving money rather than earning money through smart strategies and modernization.

Most of the processors are over dependent on masters. *"Aree usko pooch ke mill shuru ki thi kya? Itna kya darte ho"*. We constantly encourage

> **To save myself from the traditional thought process, I regularly visit international exhibitions and market, attend industry seminars, I regularly sit with knowledgeable and progressive minded people**

people to change – even from local textile industry. But they forget everything once they are out of our factory gate.

"Hamare market me tiffin culture hai. jaha negative aur mandi ki baaten zyada hoti hai aur hamara saara hosla wahi dab jata hai. Main kyu un logo ke saath baithu. Shayad isi liye humse bade aur behtar log bhi aaj humse pichhe rah gaye. Bahot se log joh aaj bahot acchha kam kar sakte hai par nahi kar pate hai". I refrain from participating in petty gossip that is integral to the "tiffin culture of our business." This demotivates us and it is because of this reason that many talented people failed to achieve the success they deserved.

To save myself from the traditional thought process, I regularly visit international exhibitions and market, attend industry seminars, I regularly sit with knowledgeable and progressive minded people. This expands my horizon; I have developed good contacts. All this has helped us develop the strong organization.

While we do this, others are not moving out of their mental frame, they are not exploring new things, new markets, new ideas etc. and as a result most of them are struggling.

We were the first company to have ISO implemented and certified. Way back in 1997-98, the govt. had a scheme to support the industry for getting organized and well managed. We grabbed that opportunity and we asked govt. to support us and provide a professional for its implementation.

Today we are in a position of such strength that visitors from Japan, Russia, Germany, South Africa. Ambassadors of different countries have visited us. They come searching for us and offer best facilities so that we can deal with companies of their countries.

More than 50 countries representatives have visited our unit, which includes textile ministers and administrative officers also. Students, traders and trade organization representatives from various cities of India also regularly visit our unit.

> *We use consultants because, as an entrepreneur we are so busy and involved in routine that we don't realize our weaknesses, problems and also the opportunities around us.*

Professional management has helped us to grow:

We have well-organized structure and each family member is having specific responsibilities.

One of my brother focuses on sales and the other on value addition department. I focus on financial management and subsidies.

We have developed small strategic units within the company, have developed sound team in each of these units, given specific targets for sales - expenses and for op.ex. & left them alone. Each operates as a separate business and produces desired results. We ask them to build their own team. We are here just as a trustee and financers.

We have deployed PWC for developing SOP for our entire operations. We have in-house and also external auditors who does the performance audit on monthly basis. We have trainers from external market which trains our team on regular basis.

Training improves team productivity, people are motivated, their loyalty towards the company grows and they respect us a lot.

We use consultants because, as an entrepreneur we are so busy and involved in routine that we don't realize our weaknesses, problems and also the opportunities around us. The consultants help us to understand them and grow. They boost our confidence and help us in making faster and yet effective decisions.

In spite of huge benefits, our entrepreneurs don't use the services of consultants because; in order to do that, first thing is to accept that they are lacking in some of the required skills and that they need help. Since they are over confident and are not willing to accept, taking professional help is a distant reality.

We gift our team members' cars and bikes for their convenience and often upgrade those vehicles from time to time. The ones who can't make

> **All 3 businesses currently are generating gross revenue of 1000 crore and target is to generate Rs.5000 crore as annual revenues in next 5 years.**

such investments on their people and right facilities, lose out on greater business values. [*Hum chalte chalte apne team members ko 25 lakh ya oos se zyada ki gaadiya de dete hai. Waqt ke sath latest gadiyan badal ke dete hai. Is waqt hamare paas company ki 25 se zyada cars and 200 se zyada bikes hai. joh is tarah facilities ke peechhe invest nahi kar sakte, who kabhi consultant, training and technology ka khul ke fayda nahi ootha sakte hai*]

Future Road Map:

Apart from Laxmipati we also have two more businesses within family. Siddhi Vinayak shipping corporation which is a shipping and infrastructure company. It has tie up with L&T for developing pvt. dock and ship repairing facility. The total cost of this project is Rs. 5000 crore

We also are into education as partner in Tapti Valley School, A day boarding school with state of art facilities.

All 3 businesses currently are generating gross revenue of 1000 crore and target is to generate Rs. 5000 crore as annual revenues in next 5 years.

In near future our plans are to enter into pharmaceutical with generic drug manufacturing and if the govt. is supportive, we also have plans for launching a college of multiple faculties

Key success factors:

If I reflect on why we succeeded? The factors that comes to my mind are; the unity in our family among all brothers has been our key strength.

Next is, we never changed our principles and policies of doing business. We have same principles since last 25 years; for customers, for employees and for suppliers and it has been always based on win-win model. We have even supported some of our dealers financially and as a result, they are loyal to us.

> ❝ I must say that, your customer is doing a favor by buying an undifferentiated product from you. ❞

Another factor for our success has been that we have complete value chain in-house, and are not dependent on any external vendor for any of our production process.

Most businesses in textile are inefficient because you are dependent on external vendors and don't have control over the value chain or supply chain. The suppliers cheat you or make false commitments and you have no choice. Same products and designs are offered to several traders by your vendors. As a result, 720 people have boarded in a coach with capacity of 72 passengers. You have no differentiation factor.

In such scenario, I must say that, your customer is doing a favor by buying an undifferentiated product from you.

This also leads to commoditization where you get lower margins, you have to give long credits to your dealers, your goods return ratio is higher, stagnant sales and low profits against applied capital. All this eats away your confidence and profits.

Social benefits from this business:

A fix portion of our annual profit goes towards social contribution. We have donated for creation of big multi facility hospitals, charitable trusts, stem cell banks, for CCTV project of the city, towards traffic brigade formation for traffic management in the city, for opening generic drug stores. Etc.

And above all we are very sensitive and critically focused on environment. As mentioned earlier, we look for opportunities to save water and other resources. Even if those solutions are expensive, we invest on them.

Our involvement in other social activities are many. My father takes care of all social work and contributions. We are invited for meetings with govt. and its various officials at-least once in a month.

> ❝ *Family ka support nahi hai, toh vyapar ka koi matlab nahi hai, woh aapko kabhi khushi nahi dega. Hamesha family ka poora khayal rakhe.* ❞

We are involved with mantra, CII, SGCCI, Mahaveer hospital, chhaydo [a local NGO working for the access to quality health services for needy people. esp. for critical illness], Sarvajanik Education Society etc.

One of the important act we do is, we invite students from young engineering colleges to see our machines that we have imported or developed in collaboration with other expert countries. We encourage these young engineers to develop local machine or models so that their practical knowledge and skills get developed as well as the local industries can get the benefits from low cost prototypes.

Our contribution towards the growth of textile industry is very meaningful. Through all these developments, we are portraying a good image of our industry and Surat city in international market. People from international markets are willing to work with Surat companies and even technology providers and latest machine manufacturers are approaching us and are willing to deal with us. At one point of time, they were avoiding us or insulting us.

Today we are the largest importer from japan in textile sector. Recently we have developed a colour mixing robotic machine at the cost of Rs.10 crores with the help of Japanese company Tsushin Kogyo. This machine saves water and chemical waste in considerable amount. People come to us to see our machines and technologies to learn from us. Somehow we have become a role model for them. I am happier about this and thus, we share our ideas and knowledge more freely with all.

Balancing is important to be happy:

I am equally careful in my personal life. I spend quality time with my parents and my wife every day. *'Family ka support nahi hai, toh vyapar ka koi matlab nahi hai, woh aapko kabhi khushi nahi dega. Hamesha family ka poora khayal rakhe'.*

> *“Log agar apni arthi per ho aur waha par bhi oose do bateen sikhne ko mile, toh sikh leni chahiye”*

Learning is critical:

My mentors are people who failed in front of us *"waqt badalta gaya aur hamare role models hi fail ho gaye, aur shayad sab se zyada unki galtiya aur failure se humne sikha"* [with times our role models started failing in business. Infact we have learnt more from their failures and mistakes]

'*Hamari industry me kuchh bahot hi acchhhe log the aur woh log sikhana bhi chahte the, humne unse bhi bahot sikha. Log fail kyon gaye, yehi hamara constant study ka focus raha hai*'. [Why people failed is the matter of constant study for us]

Constant learning is critical to success. On learning, my view is very straight; *"Log agar apni arthi per ho aur waha par bhi oose do bateen sikhne ko mile, toh sikh leni chahiye"* [even if you are on your death bed and have an opportunity to learn something, you should learn] never stop learning.

Legacy and image that I want to leave behind: I want to be a role model who created positive business and image amidst the negative environment and poor infrastructure.

My advice to other entrepreneurs is:

- Believe in yourself. Respect your suppliers as well as your buyers. [*Humne joh kiya who poore aatma vishwas ke saath kiya*. Thus we advise people *"joh karo, poore aatma vishwas ke saath karo. Grahak ki hi tarah apne supplier ka bhi bahot sanman karo. woh aapse bahot nayi baaten share kar sakta hai aur wahi jankari aapko next level per pahocha sakti hai"*]
- Don't copy others, learn from them get inspiration from them but do better than them
- Never break your commitments – even if you face some losses
- Take full advantage of all the available technologies to grow lean and fast

Y(E)ARNING FOR THE RIGHT TECHNOLOGY

Mr. Chandrakant Gondaliya
Director

Firm Name:
Aalidhra Textile Engineering Ltd.

Estd: 1975

Products or Services:
Manufacturer of various textile machines - Yarn manufacturing

It all started out as a repair workshop and currently stands as a pioneer in the textile machine manufacturing industry. Gondalia family has led this company to the zenith of success, following the footsteps of its founder Mr. Hansraj Gondalia. Today, Aalidhra is a name synonymous to supreme quality Indian machines and is an ever expanding venture.

Aalidhra Textile Engineering Ltd.

"Aalidhra today through its DTY machines and other value added yarn processing machines, enjoys the global leadership in providing cost effective POY processing technology."

.... Chandrakanth Gondaliya

It was a warm afternoon when I met Mr. Chandrakant at his office located at Udhna, Surat. He is a mechanical engineer by qualification and is in his late 40's. Currently he is heading the textile machine manufacturing division of Aalidhra group, which has several other businesses.

He mentioned that the Group was founded in 1975 by Hansrajbhai, his uncle and current chairman of the group. He was the only qualified person in the family, an electrical engineer. Rest all were farmers

Hansrajbhai started the business in 2000 sq. ft. rented premise with manufacturing and servicing of electromagnetic equipment for textiles and medical equipment. In 1982, with the entry of other family members in business, we started textile engineering with twisting (two for one twisters) and winders for different applications.

In 1985, we stared manufacturing of jacquard and sizing machines. We had three separate divisions by that time:

> **“** We did not had enough money to spend on R&D. It was like the company had resources to produce bicycle and we were trying to develop a four wheeler vehicle. **”**

1. Electrical Engineering for Textile
2. Jacquard and Sizing Division
3. Twisting Machine Division.

My entry in business:

I joined the business in 1994, after the completion of mechanical engineering from Bangalore University, in jacquard and sizing division. Which had turnover of 6 crores at that time.

In 1995, just after one year of my joining, we launched 100% indigenously developed texturizing machine. We were the first to develop this in India. Only Himson group was dealing in this technology but in foreign collaboration.

This was a first major learning phase of my life and I was given the responsibility of R&D of this high tech draw-texturizing machine. I was afraid because we did not had enough resources to manage this project. There was no manpower with core designing knowledge for this and no standard operating systems to carry out such R&D project, because no such technology was ever developed in India.

We did not had enough money to spend on R&D. It was like the company had resources to produce bicycle and we were trying to develop a four wheeler vehicle. Thus, we had to work on very tight budget, apply ourselves and do all the major work on our own with no one to delegate. We had to learn it all on our own through trial and error method and achieve excellence.

This proved as a blessing in disguise. It was a wonderful learning experience and it taught us a lot. The learning's and capabilities that we got through this project has helped this organization in many ways.

We further kept on upgrading and improvising on this technology and thus Aalidhra today through its DTY machines and other value added

> *We knew that we can offer new machines at the cost of 2nd hand imported machines and that too 100% Indian with all local service and maintenance support*

yarn processing machines, enjoys the global leadership in providing cost effective POY processing technology.

Expansion:

By the year 2000, few more members of the family joined the group and we started manufacturing polyester yarn. Here also, we launched CP [continuous polymerization] technology for the first time in India, again indigenously developed in house.

In 2010, we entered into developing and manufacturing high speed weaving machines like waterjet and rapier looms through our engineering division. This again was our own indigenous development, developed first time in India.

We developed all these technologies because we saw lot of imports of textile technology in India and also that some of the local players were importing 2nd hand machines to save cost. We knew that we can offer new machines at the cost of 2nd hand imported machines and that too 100% Indian with all local service and maintenance support.

Current Status:

Today our Gross annual revenue for Aalidhra group is 1250 crores. 500 crores comes from textile machine manufacturing and Yarn processing is generating 750 crore business.

We are very happy and satisfied with what we have achieved so far, and with all the R&D and solutions that we have delivered to the textile industry.

Currently two generations are working together. We are at five locations in textile engineering division. 10% to 15% of textile machine revenue is from exports.

Total team strength is of 500 people in engineering & approx. 700 in spinning. Total 1200 people.

> **People in many countries have not heard about shuttle looms and 90% of our weavers in India use this outdated technology. All this is Painful**

We are also into sugarcane farming and have 400 acres of farm.

Soon we are venturing into pharmaceutical business. We are the investment partners in a medicine manufacturing company at Baroda, Gujarat.

We are seven people from family working for this group, my father is the eldest. Two people are involved in spinning business, four in engineering division and uncle is the group chairman. I am the 3rd as per age sequence among all 6 brothers.

We sell approximately 100 different machines of multiple price range. With our major focus on value added technology, we want to work with challenging technologies and avoid basic routine work.

Future Plans:

India is lagging behind in textile technology. People in many countries have not heard about shuttle looms and 90% of our weavers in India use this outdated technology. All this is Painful. Our focus is to upgrade the weaving industry by providing advance technology at affordable cost.

Our vision is to be the one stop provider of all possible machines in weaving and textile related technology so that our country should not import any machines from other advance countries. Currently we have just 20% of the products in our basket. There is a huge potential and gap in textile technology, which we want to fill in coming years.

As manufacturing companies are growing, they are searching for advance technologies and are willing to pay for it. This opens up lot of potential for high-end technology also.

A clear mission with which we all are operating is to work hard intelligently and effectively for creating world-class technologies that can improve the textile industry and make it more competitive globally. All this with Indian pricing to ensure the techno commercial viability of our products.

> **“** All our family members have started from grass root level, we never get the ready chair or authority. This is an important part of our family rules. **”**

We always work on techno-commercial aspects – if our machine or technology cost is high, it will not help the industry. Thus we don't sell it.

Our Core values which we follow in every decision we take or every system or policy we make are; fair business policies, never doing anything wrong or cheating anyone - be it your staff, suppliers or customers and lastly, maintaining a hardworking nature.

Key Success Factors:

Our key success factors have been mainly the unity in family, Strong on business ethics and policies, continuous support, guidance and encouragement from our senior family members, R&D, curiosity to learn about new technologies from all possible sources and above all, good teamwork among all the family members including the professionals working with us.

Normally there are lot of disputes and difference of opinion in family managed businesses but that is not the case with us, Because of our key strengths, understanding, clear processes and certain practices.

We all are qualified engineers, all of us have clear understanding about our job role within specific business area. We don't interfere in each other's work. We have a clear understanding that all can't be same, so there is no comparison among us and we don't judge the IQ of anyone based on the business figures.

All our family members have started from grass root level, we never get the ready chair or authority. This is an important part of our family rules. In fact, the son of the chairman Hansrajbhai, my uncle who trained me, has been trained by me. He has to follow all the instructions given and work at grass root level.

We will never give them direct chair without preparing them well, without training them from the bottom.

> *We had tight financial control within the group. For investments, for cost, for R&D and for self-expenses. This taught us a lot about financial discipline and efficiency*

We are creating new businesses in diverse fields so that we can offer each member of the family an independent business.

Management and risk taking has somehow been in our DNA, we did not have to learn it from elsewhere. Engineering is more systematic and process driven study that shapes your mind and makes it process driven. We all are qualified engineers and this factor works in our favor.

Hard work, risk taking & constant learning are critical requirement for success in business.

We took a big leap in 1995 and had no idea about how to manage? The product was high end and cost per machine was 1.5 cr. To manufacture and sell it, was quite challenging and risky. To prove our ability to carry out such mighty project, I used to work for avg. 14 hours a day in those days, on Sundays too. And yes learning from all possible sources and people is what helped us.

We had no one to follow; and had to learn everything on our own. No manpower, no agency to support, no technicians, no experts and no one within family also was experienced enough. Yet, we could do it, just because we were open to new learning's.

I used to go to big companies and meet knowledgeable people and learn a lot from them by interacting and through observations.

At times, a little ignorance is also important in business. Developing texturizing machine worth 1.5 cr., on our own was a big achievement. I was young and given this project, did not know anything. In fact, it was good that I did not know anything, or else I must have never taken that project on hand. Not knowing was a boon at that time.

Knowledge and Insights are must:

Learning and penetration into any subject is extremely important because apart from costing's and R&D, we also need designs, new methods of

> *Whatever may be the problem or issue, I will approach a problem and observe a lot and that observation itself led me to most of the solutions and learning*

manufacturing, assembling, service, metallurgy, etc. and optimization in each aspect is critical.

Mastery over any one aspect will not help much. In weak competition era or high demand market it might work, but not when the going gets tough.

Other small companies don't grow beyond certain point because they lack devotion to the subject or deeper penetration. Superficial knowledge will not lead you to success.

What differentiates us from others?

Key difference between others and us has been our patient penetration for deeper knowledge and insights, great focus on quality, assurance for 100% replacement and good after sales service. An additional factor that helps us is less number of competitors, as there are not many players who would invest in R&D as we did.

We have grown in leaps and bounds and yet not much marketing efforts has been required for our sales. Only 5 people in sales team bring all the business for us because our products and it performance is our marketing.

Customers faith has been extremely good up to a level that they bought 1.5 crore machine from a new developer and that too Indian. They knew that if the machine is not working Hansrajbhai has the guts to take it back.

Use of modern technology is extremely important and that is one big differentiator between us and all other competitors. We are using ERP software for our internal management, which was developed as per the need of our business. We studied SAP but it was costly, yet I invested my time, understood it thoroughly, learnt as much as I can about it and got our own software developed which we are using since 2004.

> **Hard work, risk taking & constant learning are critical requirement for success in business.**

This helped us in precision and inventory management. we have approx. 15000 parts used in a particular machine and to manage it all is not easy. 100 crore turnover of Engineering is equal to 1000 crore turnover of processing.

By studying about SAP, we also learnt a lot about production management processes and that has helped us a lot.

We do considerable amount of outsourcing as that allows us to focus on our strengths and as well as it saves lot of capital investments. Our all 'A' class accuracy components are made in-house and rest are outsourced [We outsource and assemble approx. 40% of our total production output]

Financial discipline is very important. We had tight financial control within the group. For investments, for cost, for R&D and for self-expenses. This taught us a lot about financial discipline and efficiency [budgetary limitations did not allow us to be casual]. As a result, today we are lean, have lesser inventory, low wastage, low cost and very high focus on sourced material quality.

Managing people is managing success:

For team management our approach and process has been very simple. We deeply acknowledge that they do everything and I focus on expansion and new developments. Without team you can't grow beyond certain point.

We delegate with full authority and thus they enjoy their work. We have 1200 people and no HR department, never felt the need.

We avoid unproductive meetings and unwanted processes or interactions. We give targets and task's; the systems tell us whether the work is done or not. You don't have to report.

To get the best performance from the team, we also have to train and coach them effectively. Recently we have taken help of lean consultants to train our people and re-organize our manufacturing processes.

> **Use of modern technology is extremely important and that is one big differentiator between us and all other competitors.**

We know a lot but don't have time to execute and since the consultants work in organized manner and deal with team with structured process, it saves our time, deliver desired results and bring faster change.

Self-Management and learning:

One of the most critical aspect of our success is Learning. I Don't read much; I have read only few books on Management, but have learnt more by observations. Whatever may be the problem or issue, I will approach a problem and observe a lot and that observation itself led me to most of the solutions and learning. I have a habit of always questioning myself and challenge my knowledge.

I believe Education is extremely important for all humans: It makes a man and its knowledge systematic and it brings maturity in us.

I maintain a very balanced and healthy routine: I Get up at 6.30 and go for regular exercise. My first half at office is permanently dedicated towards meeting with customer service head and know the market feedbacks and for checking accounts and legal issues. Post lunch I spend my time with design department for new developments. Designing and customer service [timely installation] are two critical departments with whom I spend my major time.

Leave office by 7pm, go for walk, and be with family. Towards the end of the day I watch more of a history or scientific programs before going to sleep.

Family plays an important role in entrepreneurial journey:

Without family support, you can't concentrate on your business. If you have no hurdle from the family side, you can give your best shot at business. During business hours, I hardly receive 1 to 2 calls from home in a year.

> *"We believe that our contribution through our business has been very meaningful: We brought best global technology at low cost, Saved power through energy efficient machines and prevented imports by providing local solutions"*

Purpose of doing business:

We run this business because we enjoy doing it a lot. Through our business, we could work for the betterment of the textile industry, prevent lot of foreign currency drain by preventing imports, created lot of employment, we created opportunities for our people to grow in life, achieved self-growth and above all we are in a position to contribute in social development due to our capacities and prosperity.

For textile industry we developed new machines, that were never launched in India. Our machines are saving lot of power, approx. 2000 machines today are saving 50KW power per machine. We reduced the cost of machines by developing 100% Indian version of the best available technology elsewhere.

All these contributions were possible only because of the business. Had we not been into this business, we might have lived an average mediocre life. We are thankful to god for all this.

We believe that our contribution through our business has been very meaningful: We brought best global technology at low cost, Saved power through energy efficient machines and prevented imports by providing local solutions [People were importing old machines due to high cost, we gave them new machines at same cost. We also have supplied machines worth 150 crores to Reliance, if Reliance does not import, who else will?]

Our target is to stop complete imports in the segments we deal.

Social contribution:

We have family managed trust which has developed and is managing a school from 5th standard to residential college. A big hostel project is coming at kamrej and we are major contributor in that project. My wife is a doctor and since last 17 years; she works for charitable cause for half day.

My role model is my uncle Hansrajbhai and other leading organizations like Batliboi, Reliance etc. from whom, I learnt a lot in my initial days.

Advice to other entrepreneurs:

- Work hard, penetrate into the subject, Don't look to make quick money, add value.
- Work for betterment and improvement of the industry
- Be united and connected with your family. If possible, stay or work with joint family.
- Always target market leadership. Out of 100 companies in the same industry, if you are among top 10, your risk reduces considerably. You have relatively lesser problems or risk

CONSTRUCTING MAGIC

magicrete
magic behind happy homes

Mr. Sourabh Bansal
MD & Co- Founder

Firm Name:
Magicrete Building Solutions Pvt. Ltd.

Estd: 2008

Products or Services:
Manufacturer of AAC Blocks

For Mr. Sourabh Bansal, a huge order of a particular client at his family owned lime and other chemical processing plant, changed his worldview. He revolutionized the construction industry by initiating the production of AAC blocks, the latest technology in the construction industry. With the passionate efforts of an IIT graduate, Mr. Sourabh, his brother Siddharth [IIT, IIM Lucknow] and Puneet [partner's son] Magicrete is able to boost the business to about 150 crores INR of annual turnover. This is a story of dream, hard work and professionalism.

Magicrete

"My father had a foresight and he insisted that the future is of technology and technocrats will have a better future"

.... Sourabh Bansal

Mr. Sourabh Bansal recalls how his father was a director of exports with a textile firm and later on he started his own business venture. This is how the DNA of entrepreneurship started developing within his family, the DNA which gave birth to Magicrete.

I was helping my father in business and its processes since I was in class 10 and this is where I developed this whole mindset of creating my own business and not to take up a job and work for others.

I was inclined towards commerce because I wanted to start my own business but my father had a foresight and he insisted that the future is of technology and technocrats will have a better future. Thus, I took up engineering and completed my studies from IIT Kharagpur.

Since I had no inclination for a job, my mind was always busy thinking about different business ideas. Ideas related to different techno startups and services. Ideas about solar power or about digital advertisement agency etc. but most of those ideas were revolving around one central theme 'organizing the unorganized'.

During the same period Siddharth, the younger brother was doing very well in IIT Delhi and wanted to work with consulting firm. He later

> ❝ *most of the construction projects in Europe used this product, even in china 50% of the projects used AAC blocks for construction. And India would be soon following this global trend.* ❞

on went to IIM Lucknow and also worked with Mckinsey, after completing his management studies.

After all the thought processes and research, I decided to join my dad's business of lime and other chemical processing and searched for opportunities of scaling and efficiency within the existing business. I started looking for various options of forward integration with lime. Always thinking about what can be the alternate use of lime? How can we generate greater volumes?

It is always said *'Where there is a will, there is a way'*. During the same period, I discovered that one of the customers had placed a huge order and that company was into manufacturing of AAC Blocks, used for building constructions.

I started a long research on this product and its future, it's costing, its uses, its manufacturing processes, project cost, market potential, the competition, possible challenges and hurdles etc. and came to a conclusion that though it is a capital intensive project but has a great future. The estimate market size was approx. 50,000 crores and had a very positive impact on environment. It also solved the most pressing problem of the construction industry, labor crunch.

The global trends suggested that most of the construction projects in Europe used this product, even in China 50% of the projects used AAC blocks for construction. And India would be soon following this global trend and thus I decided to jump into this business.

The project establishment cost would be around 20 crores. My brother Siddharth, then 2nd year student at IIM Lucknow, suggested me and helped me to prepare a proper project report and meet several private equity investment firms.

Though we had very ambitious plans for expansion and we were full of positive energy, the idea of PE investment did not work in favor of us.

> *Each new day was a new learning for us.*

So I finally decided to opt for angel investors. And this is how Mr. Rajesh Poddar a known person to our family trusted the project and me, and agreed to invest Rs.10 crores in our business against 70% stake. The stake portion was way too high then my expectations but I applied my practical mind and agreed to the deal. After all, it was just the beginning of my career and at that stage if somebody has agreed to invest such big amount on me and my idea was in itself a very satisfactory fact for me.

This is the time when Puneet joined the business. He was the son of one of the partners of Mr. Rajesh in some other business. So now we were three people; myself [technological background], Siddharth [Management and technology (though Siddharth joined us little later)] and Puneet [financial background] and we all three together made a good team.

The company Magicrete Building Solutions Pvt. Ltd. was incorporated in April 2008. During the same period, we were successful in convincing bank for additional loan of Rs. 10 crores. We are thankful to SBI for trusting us.

Challenges faced at early startup phase:

There were several hurdles that we faced in the initial phase and each new day was a new learning for us. I would like to mention few along with its solution.

The first hurdle that we faced was related to the construction of the factory site. We had to complete the project within 6 months and start the production. The construction started on time but due to protests from villagers around factory site on environmental issues, we had to stop the construction and shift the project to a different location, which delayed the project by 6 months.

The next challenge was of sales and marketing. The production started, but who will buy? The existing users of AAC blocks were small in numbers and that was not enough to justify our production potential.

> **❝ The comparison chart proved that the savings on steel, labor and through project completion timings were high and thus we started getting good business after this long process and learning curve. ❞**

So the obvious choice was to convert non-user into users. Convincing people to use AAC blocks instead of bricks.

This had its own challenges, bricks are used since ages and people are very comfortable with its application. For AAC blocks, people had doubts about the construction quality, strength of construction, its cost was higher than usage of bricks, plastering would be proper on this block or not? Etc. so to establish the testimony, Mr. Rajesh used the AAC blocks in one of his own construction project and then referred it to other construction companies.

Once we established the testimony, we were confident and started approaching other builders, but that is where our myths & ideologies were shattered. Buyers were not concerned with green buildings or energy efficiency. All they wanted was the real value against their investments. And they were very strong in their cost calculations for which we were not ready.

This was a very important learning experience and through this we understood the basics of selling and also about effective ways of establishing the value of our product in front of the buyer to convince them.

I realized that I need to prepare cost comparison charts against the traditional brick usage. These charts helped us to understand the other cost savings of our product and get the real cost estimates along with net value of AAC block based construction. The comparison chart proved that the savings on steel, labor and through project completion timings were high and thus we started getting good business after this long process and learning curve.

The next in the list of challenges is managing the cash flow. The market was and is credit driven, where we need to fund our customers by offering our products on credit. But the market system is unprofessional, wherein; if you have offered the goods on 7 days' credit, the money comes only after

> **"***One man can't execute all this alone and thus it was a time to build a good team.***"**

2 to 3 months. This creates financial inefficiency and cash crunch. To solve this, we created a strict collection and monitoring system. With the help of ERP, we can trace the customer records and stop delivering if previous dues are not paid.

The next challenge, utilization of our full production capacity and for that we needed to expand our sales operations to other cities like Mumbai, Baroda, Ahmedabad. One man can't execute all this alone and thus it was a time to build a good team. So I turned to my batch mates from IIT and got some of them on board. The reason I turned to them is, I knew them, we shared the same passion, and I was aware about their caliber and knew that they are best people whom I can rely on. This helped us to create a strong management team and delegate the work. Shweta, my wife who had done her MBA also came on board and applied her abilities and knowledge to the best use.

Time for expansion:

After the initial phase with inception challenges been addressed, it was time to scale. In March 2011, we reached the annual turnover of 31 Cr and we had to double our production capacity at our first factory. We established our 2nd factory next door to satisfy the demand of entire western region. Our third factory was established at Jhajjar, Haryana to cater the need of the North and Central India.

We realized that we need more funds to expand further and once again the knowledge of Siddhartha about how PE Industry operates was handy. Thus with the involvement of Siddhartha we started pitching to PE firms. In march 2013, Motilal Oswal Private Equity invested Rs. 35 crores in Magicrete.

I think there were certain parameters, which helped us to get this investment, and they are; our team quality and capabilities were extremely good. Having IIT and IIM degrees was a big advantage.

> *We have strong systems and team that manage the day to day operations of business. We at times visit our factories may be once in a quarter.*

The other parameter was rapid growth in the short span of 5 years. In march 2013, we had reached the turnover of 100 crores. Next parameter was our business plan and industry potential. And this made us a valuable company to invest in.

In March 2014 our annual turnover was 130 crores and in 2015, 150 crores. we have 2000 developers as our clients. 350 people are working with us. We have two factories at Surat and one at Jhajjgar, Haryana.

Today the entire organization from top to bottom is merit based; selection of new manpower is completely based on meritorious process. Who knows whom? Is replaced by who knows what? As a result, we have strong systems and team that manage the day to day operations of business. We at times visit our factories may be once in a quarter.

But now, since the competition is heating up, more manufacturers are entering into this business, margins are decreasing. To cater this, we are expanding into new geographical territories and also have started searching for new products; Dry mortar and pre-fabricated construction.

We anticipate the future where labor availability for onsite construction would be problem and it would be prefab everywhere.

After PE funding what has changed? Now there is a huge moral responsibility on our shoulder since they have invested money by trusting your abilities. Though there is no financial obligations and commitments made.

My next responsibility is to scale the organization to greater heights and produce better results for all the stakeholders.

We are never forced to do growth just for the sake of growth, there is a miss conception that all Pvt. Equity investors force you to go for rapid growth and pressurize you unnecessarily. This is not true. I personally met Mr. Ramdevji Agarwal the joint MD of Motilal Oswal group, which has invested in our business.

> ❝ *Your every decision should be based on the balance between the short-term returns as well as the long-term growth, stability and value creation of the organization* ❞

I asked him that since the real estate market is in recession and we have not delivered better results? Upon which he said, did I ask you to produce forceful results, or did I ever asked you how much return have you produced? No. so don't be under pressure. Do the business the way you have been doing in past 5 years and just focus on milking your existing cows. You have two manufacturing units, just try to get the best possible output from both and leave the result analysis to us. But yes, back of the mind I have this moral responsibility.

At the end of the day the value of the business depends upon the profit it produces and not upon how much revenue have you produced? Unlike the technology companies. But they too will have to answer at some point of time to the markets and investors.

Its profit that eventually matters. If the company is not debt heavy and if your operations are efficient, your growth will automatically come and you will maximize the profits.

The relationship with Pvt. Equity investors are not long term, they are not here for 20 years. They are there for 5 to 7 years. So when we make decisions we have to understand that in order to give faster and bigger returns to these PE investors you cannot sacrifice the long-term future of the company. Your every decision should be based on the balance between the short-term returns as well as the long-term growth, stability and value creation of the organization. And we are fortunate to have partners with us that understand this fact.

Present day challenges:

After achieving scale, having 350 people, more number of customers to handle and more units and resources to manage. There are certain challenges that evolve naturally.

Bigger challenge is a personal one; it is 'the inertia'. Having nothing and reaching somewhere is all together a different game and having

> **❝** *You can't interfere regularly; maybe you can coach or mentor but you can't interfere. Or else you will disturb the system from functioning effectively and you also deprive your team of learning opportunities.* **❞**

something and trying to move further is different. Though you have access to all the resources, can you sustain the same energy level, does the agility prevail and can you sustain the same passion? This is why some people don't grow beyond certain point of achievement in business.

Next is dropping agility. Decisions and action used to be much faster in early days, since you were the decision maker. But today there are hierarchies and the respective heads are the decision makers, there are lot of processes to follow to reach every decision and that reduces the speed and agility. Not all departments will go at same pace. Ensuring the productivity of the organization amidst this system is a major challenge.

You know that certain systems are not going right or functioning in a right manner but you have to stay out by choice and allow people to function and then learn from their own mistakes. You can't interfere regularly; maybe you can coach or mentor but you can't interfere. Or else you will disturb the system from functioning effectively and you also deprive your team of learning opportunities.

Another challenge is managing the diversity of ideas and opinion; one of the reasons of our progress is that the board has shown lot of trust in the ability of leaders and have given them the necessary freedom to make decisions. The hierarchy is very clear at all levels, which helps the enterprise to take right decisions. The board doesn't interfere in day-to-day decision-making. We have a clear governance structure in place.

This is the problem with most of the growing organizations; they don't have proper organization structure. Multiple reporting authorities, multiple tasks, lot of personal ego etc. effects the progress and the smooth functioning of the business and thus they don't grow beyond certain point

In my opinion, why most of the MSME's don't grow beyond certain point? Esp. after the entries of 2nd or 3rd generations are that their ideas are not accepted or respected.

> **The problem with most of the businesses is that the older generation is not willing to re-invent themselves and the new generation is unable to understand the context from which these previous generation entrepreneurs are coming from**

I saw my dad doing lot of hard work in business and that is the very reason why I don't want to do the business the way he did it. That does not mean, what he did was not right. He was absolutely right in his context. He operated in an environment where infrastructure was weak, availability of right talent was tough and the technology was not developed. Hence their involvement in business was much more draining and it was at the cost of personal and family life.

I want a well-balanced and peaceful life along with running a business and today there are resources, information, knowledge, and technology to support you. I find no reason why one should sacrifice their personal life for the business.

Due to rising literacy in India, today we have access to educated manpower and we have all the best technologies available, transportation and basic infrastructure is also better and we should use it to the fullest.

The problem with most of the businesses is that the older generation is not willing to re-invent themselves and the new generation is unable to understand the context from which these previous generation entrepreneurs are coming from. Fortunately, we had no such issues.

Learning through business:

Key learning from my entrepreneurial journey so far has been that you must have great team selected with merit based criteria, initially there were people who came through references but they disturbed the systems and had created inefficiencies and problems. Your recruitment process has to be very strong and transparent – don't rely on your judgment about people's ability, let them pass through the right processes and let the system assess them.

> ❝ *'Garbage in - Garbage out'. If you don't feed your system with qualitative and effective data and information, it will produce nothing for you.* ❞

Technology is the key to growth:

Use of right technology and management systems is also critical for scaling. The way we operated in initial years and the system with which we operate today is completely different.

Technology has been one of the major reasons for our success and one of our key differentiation factor. We use ERP, EI tools, we use Business Analytics Tools, we operate on Microsoft's Navision and our sales management happens through the technology. All reporting and data base management is happening with software support. We have supply chain and CRM modules very active in our ERP. We have HR info. system for all HR functions, we have GPRS tracking for all our vehicles to track the real time status of our deliveries.

Customer retention has increased because of the technology. Even our team's loyalty has grown. We are in a position to make effective decisions. Our delivery time has reduced from 18 hours to 6 hours. It helped us to deliver better service to our customers.

My system will not accept the poor quality material, my system does not allow the goods receive note if the QC department has not approved the quality.

As soon as our truck leaves our plant our customers receive the message with all the necessary details, which earlier they had to call and ask us repeatedly.

'Garbage in - Garbage out'. If you don't feed your system with qualitative and effective data and information, it will produce nothing for you. We feed our system with qualitative data and hence it produces valuable insights for us.

Not necessary that the technology has to be expensive but yes it should be simple and should support your business processes effectively.

> *"Our precast services will build house for our customers within 60 days' time and above all the cost and time of the project would be fixed."*

Define your vision and mission:

To succeed, organizations must operate with a clear vision and mission: We have a clear mission of providing innovative construction technology to Indian construction industry. This has been our focus area and we want to lead this industry. We want to change the way how things are happening

Value creation through our business:

We are increasing Energy efficiency, Time and Labor efficiency and Reducing production time and cost. This will always remain as our prime focus areas.

Our dry mix product saves time, energy, water and labor dependency. And AAC blocks are greener building material & requires only one fifth of the labor that is consumed by the traditional construction method.

Our present product portfolio comprises of AAC blocks, Magic bond, Dry mix, Plasters factory mix, Magic Putty plus and Precast.

We have recently developed an application 'buildmyghar.com' where villa's would be designed from our portal and construction would be executed by us using precast material. Our precast services will build house for our customers within 60 days' time and above all the cost and time of the project would be fixed.

Future Growth Plans:

Vision and responsibility goes hand in hand: When I was in college, business for me was just about numbers. The new techno startups were raising funds and growing faster.

> ❝ You can grow only as far as your vision is but beyond certain point, your vision alone can't take the organization further. It is the team that drives it ahead. ❞

Even I dreamt about creating a billion-dollar organization but as I got into the real time business and got involved, I realized that business is much more than just numbers and it is not just about your dream. It is all about collective vision of the team. It's about every one's dream, about every person who have joined you. So the focus shifts with time.

Today there are some 800 to 900 families associated with us and we have the responsibility to think about the benefit of all. And that has become one of the important objectives behind running this business.

It is no more about chasing numbers. Off course we have certain numbers as a milestone to achieve. But the objective is much greater.

As per our initial plans, by now we should have 10 factories. That plan was developed by a 25 years old young who did not had any idea about the realities of business. Who thought that life will always be kind to us, that the markets and economy will always favor us? But now we are operating as per the market trends. Yet; our vision very much remains the same and we are still chasing those numbers but with a greater sense of responsibility.

Role of our team in our success:

I would say that all the success till date is due to our team. You can grow only as far as your vision is but beyond certain point, your vision alone can't take the organization further. It is the team that drives it ahead. Beyond certain point you are nothing but a visionary for the company. It is only when your team is aligned with your vision that your organization produces the desired results.

You need people who are better than you, they should be expert in each function. Delegate to them, empower them, encourage inter team

> **There are 3 types of infrastructure in an organization: Physical infrastructure – Intellectual infrastructure – Emotional infrastructure. Out of which the third one is missing from most of the organizations**

interaction so that all moves in a common direction, and coach them all.

For team to perform better, first provide and communicate the right vision, equip them with right resources and enabling environment. Provide necessary motivation, be in touch and understand their challenges and help them to solve it for themselves, have an engaged team, also have a proper feedback mechanism in place.

There are 3 types of infrastructure in an organization:

- Physical infrastructure – that is furniture fixture and facilities and assets
- Intellectual infrastructure – team's ability and knowledge
- Emotional infrastructure - bonding of the team with the organization

Out of which the third one is missing from most of the organizations and thus there is no attachment, no sense of ownership and people are focused only on their respective growth. We are taking great care of this and working very hard to sustain all three aspects.

Family plays an important role in our success:

No one would be successful without the support of the family. For me my first and biggest supporter has been my father as he himself was an entrepreneur and knew the challenges of building and enterprise. My mom is a biggest contributor towards my education, she took great care to ensure that we receive right nurturing.

After marriage my wife too has been one of the greatest support. She is taking care of all responsibilities at the family and social front and

> **You need to deal with people, you need to source funds, you need to hire smarter people and for all this, your upgradation and learning is extremely critical.**

taking good care of my kids and above all having a good understanding towards my own challenges and my unreasonable involvement in the business

Entrepreneurs must constantly learn and search for something new:

Learning is very much the integral part of an entrepreneur's life. You need to know about technology, about management, about economy, about finance, about the markets, about building relationships. You also need to network a lot and learn from others. Books are important sources and of course these days googling is also a major source.

To me, the IIT degree has helped a lot in many ways but that is just a degree and is not sufficient. The knowledge has a very superior role to play in an entrepreneur's life. You need to deal with people, you need to source funds, you need to hire smarter people and for all this, your upgradation and learning is extremely critical.

We have made significant investments in R&D. Smaller organizations can't spend too much in fundamental research, but they surely can learn the best practices of others and modify them, improve them and implement them into their businesses. Which they should do?

With the intentions to help the freshers, we invite lot of interns and give them motion study or boiler performance study or automation project, this helps both of us. They help us in lot of analytical aspects and in return they get lot of practical knowledge which will help them to shape their careers.

I am inspired by many but to name a few; Bansal's of flipKart, Bhavesh Agarwal of OLA Cabs & Tata's because they have created a value based enterprise.

My advice other entrepreneurs are:

- Think big.
- Organizations are built by great teams with great systems built around them so work towards building good quality team and systems and keep innovating
- Differentiate yourself and deliver greater value to entire eco system. Today the competition is fierce and thus you need to constantly work on differentiating yourself from others and create extra value then what your competitors are doing.

ONE CAP, MANY FEATHERS

Mr. Keyur Kheni

CEO

Firm Name:

Hindva

Estd: 1988

Products or Services:

Diamonds, constructions, hospitality and textiles

Migrating from a small village of Saurashtra, loaded with big dreams, Kheni and Patel Family, led by respective Shri Manjibhai M. Patel, Shri Pravinbhai M. Kheni, Shri Himmatbhai M. Kheni and Shri Mukeshbhai M. Patel, started a diamond-polishing unit at Surat, named M. Kantilal Exports and scaled it to popularity within no time. Today their business group 'Hindva' is a diverse conglomerate having ventures in the real estate, mines, textiles, diamonds, hospitality and health care. Hindva is currently one of the well-known names in construction industry.

Hindva

"Your Vision leads society to witness the great inventions"

- Keyur Kheni (Managing Director – Hindva Group)

Diamond as a business is not older than 150 years. In past, diamonds and gold were only for kings and royal families, completely out of reach of the common man.

The British were the only ones who had a clear system and module with which they ruled half of the world. They did 200 years of a mining contract in Africa and took those diamonds to UK. The oldest company of the world is a British firm.

World's first diamond polishing company was started in Amsterdam and the Britishers had complete value chain from mining to polishing. But after the World War II, it was difficult to maintain and post freedom era Surat was rising to take this as opportunity and therefore, Surat became a hub of Diamond polishing unit that every 9 out of 10 polished diamonds in the world are from city self.

Mr. Keyur Kheni the 2nd generation member of the family owned business recalls the entire journey of the Hindva Group.

> **❝** In 2005, we also invested in couple of the projects of Mumbai based 'Lodha' group, we bought the apollo mill with them. **❞**

We were initially farmers in Saurashtra, but water scarcity forced us to move out of our villages. We are from Bhavnagar district and it had major crisis of water. At the same time, the word about Surat's diamond polishing work was viral in Saurashtra and its payment was lucrative so lot of people travelled to Surat to explore. My uncle was one of them. This was in early 70s.

My father, and uncles started diamond-polishing unit after few years of working as a labor. Their risk taking spirit was high and they wanted to do something big. They started with one ghanti and immediately established 100 ghanti within no time.

100 ghanti in such short time was big news in our villages and loads of people came to work with us. We were one of the pioneers who established the diamond industry in Surat.

Surti people in those days and even today believed in earning, spending & enjoying life. Whereas the Kathiawadis at that time believed in hardworking, earning and risking more with reinvestments in business expansion and diversification. So they saved their earnings and invested in businesses rather than spending.

We had 100 ghantis between the years 1978 to 89. Later they planned to expand further and thus created a big factory by 1992 with 3000 ghantis. This scaled the production capacity to a great extent.

> ❝ After 2008 it was the clear decision that we will create our own brand and no more investments in other construction companies. ❞

Around in year 2000, My father decided to diversify and got active in real estate business. This is how we ventured into the real estate.

The word HINDVA always attracted us, it exudes an Indian feel, it is also the alternate name of God Ramdev Pir – 'Hindva Pir'.

Expansion in Construction Business:

Today HINDVA is one of the leading name in real estate market of Surat and the reason behind it is that we have developed some unique projects.

Our venture, 'The World Hotel' is a 320 room hotel, developed on the PPP model, is one of the unique projects. Here, the investors own the property (the hotel rooms) and get income from the generated business. It is a time-share model where they buy a hotel room as their property, but it is managed by us. We generate business for the hotel and each room owners get profit share from the generated revenue. Along with profits they get 60 nights stay free for their use. These nights can be shared with others. If you don't use, you can give it back to us at a fix price.

In short it is like owning a property and investing the property for revenue generation.

> **We are also venturing into a multispeciality hospital project 'Re-life' with the capacity of 700 beds. Our major focus will be to target medical tourism market**

We don't have any good hotel in the commercial area of Surat, where the business visitors are more. So this was very successful. We sold all 320 rooms within a short duration. We maintain the property and get the hotel business by attracting the visitors. Both keep 50-50 of the money received.

We keep the maintenance of our projects in our hand for all our projects, to ensure the quality and cleanliness of all the project.

We believe in religious harmony and respect for all faith and thus we sell our properties to one and all. Anyone belonging to any religion can buy properties in our project.

We are also venturing into a multispeciality hospital project with the capacity of 700 beds. Our major focus will be to target medical tourism market. This hospital will be located near the Lal Darwaja area of Surat.

Since 2009, we also are into the textiles business with a weaving unit for shirting's and also into soft embroidery. The products are especially created for the international market.

We have also invested in bauxite mines in 2008. It is at Jamnagar

Our current net worth value is Rs. 7400 crores, certified by interbrand International, an American agency. All our group businesses are operating under Hindva brand.

> **To ensure smooth operations and better management, each members had been given a well-defined role. Financial decisions are taken jointly and rest execution is left to individual project holder.**

At present we have 11 projects running in Surat, 5 at Ahmedabad, and SRA project at Mumbai, Kalina which will be launched this year 2017.

Current Management Structure:

Total 11 members from both the families are running the entire group businesses. 3 generations are working today hand in hand – my father, my brothers, myself and children of my brothers.

To ensure smooth operations and better management, each members had been given a well-defined role and our responsibilities are clear. We have regular meetings and discussion for the reporting and analysis purpose, thus there is no need of interfering into another project or department. Financial decisions are taken jointly and rest execution is left to individual project holder.

Future Plans:

In near future, we want to take 'The World Hotel' to Pune, Ahmedabad, and Jaipur.

We want to start construction projects in multiple cities and create a national identity for our group. Major focus would be on constructions, Textiles and Health Care.

> **❝ I read a lot. A Reader is often open-minded and has a philosophical bent. You will not find any reader to be a criminal. ❞**

We also are planning for an IPO which would be initiated once we reach to the valuation of 10,000 crore.

We want to prepare effective modules and franchise at greater scale, in whatever business we do. McDonalds is scaled because of effective management module; we desire to do the same.

People Management:

Management is all about people. You don't have to manage the machines but you have to be good at managing people. How to get the desired performance from our team is often a relevant question.

When I had joined, our team had experience of executing low-end projects. When we launched the high-end premium projects, they could not deliver the desired quality. So to train them, we sent them to multiple cities and asked them to stay in high-end hotels and see their interior and structures and experience the luxury. I also asked them to see the hotel videos on YouTube. They did so and within few weeks, they came up with excellent ideas and designs.

The learning from this episode was that if we encourage them and provide right facilities, they will perform.

Constant Learning is the Key:

To upgrade myself, I read a lot. A Reader is often open-minded and has a philosophical bent. You will not find any reader to be a criminal.

Our first generation was not educated, but they ensured that the entire 2nd generation gets education in management and administration. We all from 2nd generation have done BBA or MBA.

> **❝** Our benchmark is the TATAs. It has one of the oldest and most loyal team in corporate history. **❞**

The third generation is now moving towards architecture and civil engineering, because we need this knowledge and skill in our company.

We all fill the different skill gaps in our businesses. Some bring marketing skills, some constructions, some productions etc.

Use of software & technology:

Currently, our complete business is ERP based. We get the right data on real time and thus we make effective decision quickly. All our businesses are managed through technology.

0.75% of the total business is spent on marketing and we also make regular investments in technology upgradation and modernization.

We have invested in technology upgradation for our diamond unit, to get the best quality production and reduce dependency on human labor.

Key Success Factors:

Our family values are strong and that is our key success factor. We are very active in CSR and are very generous for meaningful cause. The other factor is the unity in the family.

Our benchmark is the TATAs. It has one of the oldest and most loyal team in corporate history. That is our focus. We want to be like them.

The other factors that has contributed to our success are; the wisdom of the first generation, the Qualified 2nd generation, timely Diversification into multiple and high potential businesses, focus on branding and creating loyal team, consistently taking calculative risk and investment in latest technologies.

> **❝** *one of my personal aspirations is that, I want to create a modern school and college in Surat. I have seen education level of UK and want to fill that gap* **❞**

We are fortunate to have all these characteristics in one group. This is helping us big time.

Social Contribution:

In our CSR activities, some of the major contributions has been: donations in Saurashtra jaldhara trust for water resources to promote agricultural output. It's a team effort of a lot of senior community members.

We have built a school in the name of grandfather, made a check dam in parvadi village, developed a Samaj bhavan at katargam. It is in the name of our grandparents. We have modernized our village, with 3 medical store running on subsidized rates.

Apart from this, one of my personal aspirations is that, I want to create a modern school and college in Surat. I have seen education level of UK and want to fill that gap. But Surat does not have that vision, people still don't think forward.

My Inspirations:

My Role model is my Father although, I have learnt a lot from the biography of 'Steve Jobs' – the inventor of Apple products. At once, I had a music player with one CD, whereas further, I saw an iPod with 1000 songs and that mesmerized me, the thinking and imagination of that man inspired me a lot. He imagined a colorful screen on the computer, he created Pixar, iPod, iPhone, iPad etc. he was very imaginative in marketing. His imagination and creation has inspired many across the world.

I advise the budding entrepreneurs to:

- Focus on technology. I went to visit Google office, in San Francisco and also visited the Apple city. At one point of time, San Francisco was like Surat with lot of natural calamity and disasters. Google collected complete data of entire city and uploaded it online so that people can get real time info about almost everything. Later they took the same concept to global scale and created the Google that we know.

- Have a clear vision. In the west, if a person starts even a small restaurant, they do it with the future in mind. They think long term and develop sound systems and modules from day one. I have seen waiter less restaurants over there. With tablet on each table, order and pay from your table and message pops once your food is ready, you go and collect your food. *Even Surat can be better than San Francisco – if we have a vision.*

- Do everything with transparency and a clear concept, develop a scalable model. Don't enter into something that you can't scale. Whenever people come to you, they should have a unique brand experience. Which is different than others.

- Digital media and social media transparency and use is must. Be aggressive in your brand promotion and for the awareness about your business.

THE F: FACTOR: Fashion with Foresight

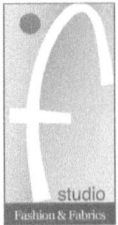

Mr. Subhash Dhawan

Founder

Firm Name:

F- Studio

Estd: 2000

Products or Services

Fashion Fabrics

Born to a family of zamindars, Mr. Subhash Dhawan a patriotic and passionate entrepreneur, always had the entrepreneurial zeal in him. He refused to be tied down to his father's textile retail stores and initiated a bolder step into the business world. His creation, Gokul Tex Fab Pvt. Ltd. & Retail Brand for natural fabrics 'F-studio' are currently, one of the popular names in the textile and the natural fabric industry, skirting a turnover of over 250 crores INR.

F-Studio

"I would always think of ways to contribute to the development of this nation through my business"

.... Subhash Dhawan

Hailing from a Zamindar family, Mr. Subhash Dhawan was not really a seasoned businessperson. But it was his vision, entrepreneurial skills and love for the nation that drove him to such heights of success.

I belonged to a zamindar family from Hajaribaugh, Jharkhand. The common perception was that the zamindars don't do business. So my grandfather used to sell properties in order to run the family but my father was against this and he decided to start his own business. Around 1954, he started as a small trader of textile products. I entered the business in 1975 and converted it into a wholesale business.

I would always think of ways to contribute to the development of this nation through my business. I realized that it was not possible to fulfill that from Hajaribaugh. Thus I shifted to Surat because I liked the way the market operated in Surat, the potential was good and it started attracting me. I am happy with whatever I have done in the last 15 years.

"The world was changing and the needs of the global market and consumer was changing as well, but Surat was still focused only on synthetic fabrics. Since, it had produced good results for them till date, so

> ❝ *Our prime focus was to pitch India as a better destination against China in textile and esp. in natural fabric trade sector.* ❞

they were not looking beyond and searching for next. We realized that the trend is moving towards natural fabric but Surat's markets were not at all taking it seriously."

I did 5 years of extensive study about Surat and the textile market. I observed that the market was not ready for global trends. I also visited China during that period and saw how their textile industry worked and what were their strengths.

That is when I discovered that pure silk is imported from China to India in large quantity and I thought it was important to prevent such imports. It was difficult to compete with china in silk as we don't produce raw silk in large quantity in India, thus we focused more on other alternatives like cotton, viscos, linen etc. which replaced silk in some manner. We opted for these fabrics because the raw material is produced in bulk in India.

Our prime focus was to pitch India as a better destination against China in textile and esp. in natural fabric trade sector. When we entered into manufacturing, I had zero experience, but we effectively managed to cover the knowledge gap, by studying the markets for 5 years and collecting the inputs from all the leading players about different aspects of fabric manufacturing and trading.

I always had a different view about the situation. Identifying the growing trend towards natural fabrics, we decided to focus on natural fabric and started our venture in the year 2000.

Naysayer said: "People produce synthetic in Surat because it is easier and the entire eco system is built around synthetic fabric. So they advised us to trade in synthetics. They argued that even the buyers too look for synthetics in Surat and you are focusing on natural fabrics? Have you gone mad? It will not work, play safe?"

The entire weaving mechanism and technology was around polyester and we wanted to go natural. So we modified the machine significantly. It

> *We were always ahead of others in our learning curve and were among the early adopters of all latest technologies in textile processing*

was very challenging, but we knew the potential, so decided to develop everything on our own.

Even in dyeing, we initially started with pot dyeing process and then we tied up with one of the local mill and convinced them to modify their processing and printing methods to support our cause. Later, when we got a good scale, we installed the digital printing machine in-house.

Now the ecosystem has accepted our innovation and up to 90% of the requirements can be satisfied from the Surat pocket itself.

First we developed the weaving unit and later, the processing facilities were developed. As a result, the imports of silk from china reduced by 80%. This is one of the major achievements for me and I am very happy about it.

We are the development partners for Aditya Birla group in natural fabrics, which is the leading brand in the Indian market in natural fabrics. We are also the dealer of Asahi Japan for India market.

We were always ahead of others in our learning curve and were among the early adopters of all latest technologies in textile processing. When digital printing was a new technology for textile, in 2005-06, we were one of the early adaptors of this technology. The other players from Surat market were still into studying and analytical phase of this technology and were still thinking, whether to invest in this technology or not? Even today, after 10 years, many are yet to adopt it.

Launch of F Studio:

We created natural fabric but did not know whether the market will accept it or not? Our fabric was mainly targeted to the fashion designers as they work on new trends, new fashion and develop new garment trends. So to test the acceptability of our products, we decided to start our own retail outlet and today we have 10 such outlets in different parts of the country.

> **" Today approximately 300 outlets of natural fabrics have started in Surat itself. Everyone drew inspiration from our success. "**

The idea has clicked well for us and helped us to create a very strong brand identity 'F-Studio'.

The first such store was at the Parle point, Surat. The reason why we chose this area was because there were approximately 15 fashion designers in that area whom we wanted to target. We got wonderful response in first 6 months.

Today approximately 300 outlets of natural fabrics have started in Surat itself. Everyone drew inspiration from our success.

Due to our efforts on fabrics like viscos, modal, linen etc. Production and demand of such fabrics has grown 10 times in last 15 years.

Gokul texprint Pvt. Ltd. is our company name, which is the manufacturing unit. It carries out weaving, dying, printing and value addition process and supplies the fabric to f-studio. F-Studio is our brand name for trading in natural fabric.

Current status and future plans:

Currently we have 10 stores of f-Studio pan India and by 2018, creating 30 stores is the target. We also supply to wholesale dealers and they supply to fashion designers.

We are focused on fabrics for female garments and 95% of our fabric is for them. 5% is for the male users. Our current processing capacity is of 10 lakh meters per month, all natural fabrics.

We are doing business worth Rs 250 crore. Gokul generates revenue of around 200 crore per annum and f-studio does approximately 50 crore. What makes this achievement meaningful is that, we had entered into a completely unknown business segment, which is developed single handedly by us in the span of 15 years.

There are many others who are following us and are dealing in the natural fabrics. So the combined market of natural fabrics in Surat is much

> **❝ I have a dream of creating a national hub for fashion designers in India. In that Hub, the top 100 fashion designers will have their stores and 50000 fashion designers will be the members. ❞**

higher. When we entered as a dealer, it was a 100-ton yarn in a year for Asahi; today it is 450 tons per annum.

We encourage new and young fashion designers a lot. We ran the 'D-Designer of Surat' contest in 2012 with the help of a radio partner, radio mirchi. later we ran the 'D-Designer of Gujarat' campaign to take it to state level where almost 5000 designers participated in that.

Recently we ran the 'D- Designer of east' contest at Kolkata and about 5000 designers from east India participated in it. Now we are looking at D-designer of west, north and south. A.V. Birla group and Asahi japan is also supporting us in this cause. By 2017 we are planning a 'D-Designer of India' Contest, on the lines of Lakme fashion week.

I have a dream of creating a national hub for fashion designers in India. If Surat has better air connectivity, it will be developed here or else it will be at some other place. In that Hub, the top 100 fashion designers will have their stores and 50000 fashion designers will be the members. And only the registered buyers can visit the hub and purchase from there. This will provide safety to designers from copy and duplication and will help them with marketing, as they will have access to genuine registered buyers.

Gokul is our own manufacturing brand, and f-studio is our retail brand. Gokul will have a significant presence in that hub. This project execution timeline is 2017-18.

On the lines of appeal by our honorable Prime minister, to manufacture zero defect products and export, we have developed such products of European quality standards and its exports has already started.

Our next focus is on producing and exporting high-end fabrics. Today high-end fabric from India is not exported; our quality is not accepted in the international markets. India is mainly in the exports of polyester and cotton fabrics. Currently we are working on the export of high-end fabrics and hopefully we would be able to do it successfully.

> **We invested a lot of money and time on R&D and experimentation. That is the only hobby or passion that I have till date.**

My children have joined me and I think very soon we will cross 1000 crore.

My elder son has been with me in this business since 5 years. My daughter in law is a fashion designer from London and helps me in innovation and R&D as per the global trends.

R&D is our passion and strength:

We invested a lot of money and time on R&D and experimentation. That is the only hobby or passion that I have till date. At times we lose lot of money behind this cause but I take it in my stride. Since we are not gambling or doing something wrong. This thought makes me comfortable with the losses. I always knew that natural fabric has an excellent future ahead and will help the entire industry and this country.

What yarn is to be mixed with what other material, is our strength and we work a lot on this aspect. With Aditya Birla, whatever new fiber is developed by them, we do R&D on it and develop new types of threads for weaving. We are their R&D partners in the market user aspect. We create new combination from multiple fibers, and making it acceptable to market is our role.

People Management:

For manpower management, our policy is; we bring people with good potential, train them on a particular aspect, make them responsible for a particular division and then we share profit percentage from their respective projects. If we don't pay well, our competitors would pay them higher amount because these people are very well trained by us.

We need to develop better management structure and better quality of team to fulfill our vision.

> **I have been invited to the institutions like chamber of commerce and also in several fashion designing institutes to speak and motivate people.**

I devote my success to our Futuristic thinking and devotion to industry, company, products and the country.

Social Activities:

I am very active in social work; I am a patriotic person since childhood and always work for it. I have created, with other likeminded people like Vinay Pathrala, a group called 'Bharat Bharti', in which people from around 24 states are members. This group works for the social equilibrium and inter religion unity. We promote patriotism a lot in this group. We provide a platform to people from different background and regions to come closer and interact and know each other and their culture.

The honorable Prime minister of India, Shri Narendra Modi, the honorable Governor and many other dignitaries have been our guest at various events. We intervene in several social disputes and try to settle things so that work can progress and social harmony is sustained.

I have been invited to the institutions like chamber of commerce and also in several fashion designing institutes to speak and motivate people.

Family Support:

Reflecting on my life, I can confidently say that, my success is due to my wife.

I got married at the age of 18. My business was 20 kms away from my home. It had no good roads or infrastructure. People were not supporting a zamindar doing business. I used to have lot of struggle and face lot of hurdles. But even in that struggling period, my wife always welcomed me at home cheerfully, even at late nights. She used to cook hot food instantly on 'chulha', since there was no gas supply or stove in those days. She has always been my strength.

Of course now my son and my daughter in law are the key drivers for all recent developments and growth and are the major contributors in our success.

I thank god for all that we have achieved so far as a family.

My Advice to other entrepreneurs is:

- "Enjoy what you do and select your profession or business carefully. Know what you are passionate about and get fully devoted to your work. In this process, you will achieve doctorate without a formal degree in your field and you will beat even the most qualified people in your sector".
- Please encourage people and your children in the field that they like; be it sports, arts or any sector of education. How much money I make should not be the criteria to select a field or a business.

POLISHING DIAMONDS, POLISHING LIVES

Mr. Hitesh Patel

Chairman

Firm Name:

DRC System India Pvt. Ltd.

Dharmanandan Diamonds Pvt. Ltd.

Estd: 1991

Products or Services

Polishing, Trading And Exports Of Diamonds And Diamond Jewelry

As the second generation entrepreneurs, Mr. Hitesh Patel & his cousin brother's major challenge was to upgrade the initiative taken by their founders from first generation & modernize their business to make it contemporary. From introducing latest technology, to including bank funding in the process of production, they gave the business a new leash of life. Today, Dharmanandan Diamonds has an annual turnover of 5000 crores INR and is all set for further expansion

Dharmanandan Diamonds

"Our USP has been Quality control; we have never experimented with the cutting and the quality just for the sake of higher profits. We were so famous for our quality that DD cut was like a benchmark for the industry."

.... Hitesh Patel

Laljibhai Patel, my father and Tulsibhai, his childhood friend, founded the business in 1975. Both studied at Rajkot in Swaminarayan gurukul. The name of the company in initial years was Shreeji Gems, which was later renamed as Dharmanandan diamond in 1993.

Both the founders had a thought that Surat is a good place to work and thus they came to Surat. Initially my father worked as labor and Tulsi kaka as a supervisor in the local diamond-polishing unit. In 1975 they decided to take a plunge into the business and started with a small capital, 2 ghantis & lot of hope and self-belief.

Expansion Phase:

The initial years of business were about establishing and steady, moderate growth. It is when the 2nd generation started entering the business from early 90's and I joined in 1997 that we started growing exponentially. The younger generation brought fresh perspectives and ideas, increased

> *" as we entered the business, we realized that, in order to scale fast and achieve rapid growth, we need to invest in modern technologies for better production, in management systems & in marketing and sales efforts. "*

the use of modern technology which has helped the organization in rapid growth.

The 2nd generation, which was very young, brought some major changes in several aspects of the business, did makeover for this company and gave it a new look.

Key changes since the year 2000 were mainly into 4 major areas, Firstly, we sourced bank funding. Second, we increased the use of modern technology in production and management. Third, we developed the better quality team. Finally, we increased our focus on sales and marketing.

Our founders always believed in self-funded business with zero debt. And since our suppliers were good and offered us rough diamonds on credit, this helped us to manage our working capital. This system helped us to achieve a steady, moderate growth and that was crucial at that point of time. As we entered the business, we realized that, in order to scale fast and achieve rapid growth, we need to invest in modern technologies for better production, in management systems & in marketing and sales efforts.

We discussed this with our seniors and convinced them to go for bank funding.

Since our goodwill was high, the bank offered us the loan of Rs. 50 crores, but we borrowed only Rs. 5 crores, which was sufficient for us. Anything excess is poisonous and that also causes a lot of inefficiencies and mismanagement. Thus, we decided to be prudent and borrowed less.

We invested most of those funds into modern machines for diamond planning and polishing and in software for better management of an entire business.

Sarin was a good technology for diamond planning. As I came to know about it, we asked for a demo, which we got after a month. Within 3 days

> **Earlier, the manufacturing was considered as the major driver but today since the production has grown, sales and marketing have become the major driver of the business.**

of demo, I realized the benefits of that technology and decided to go for it. But the cost of each machine was very high, each machine was costing us up to INR 25 lakhs.

Again the traditional thought was that the technology is expensive and we should not give lot of money for it. We convinced our seniors to shift their mindset from what we are paying, to what we are getting. We strongly insisted on the benefits of Sarin to our business and convinced them for the purchase. We were among the first customers for Sarin in Surat. Today we have 300 such units.

Later we went for manufacturing process management software – we have the in-house team of software designers who work on the in-house ERP. We invest approximately 40 to 50 lakh rupees per annum in maintaining and upgrading software and technology.

Today we have the highest number of green machines in Surat, which is the latest development for diamond polishing technology. We don't do it to show others, rather the whole focus is on what benefits it can produce for us.

Once the fund and technology related issues were solved, the next focus was on developing a better quality team. And the better quality of manpower comes at higher cost. Here again, the traditional thought and trend in the entire industry were to hire people at lower cost– we broke that myth and brought good quality people and paid them better. As a result, we started working on bigger diamonds and our growth escalated due to this.

All the above changes brought professionalism in production and business management.

The next step was to focus on sales and marketing.

Earlier, the manufacturing was considered as the major driver but today since the production has grown, sales and marketing have become the major driver of the business.

> **❝ My father and Tulsi kaka always advised us that if you trust someone, trust fully. Be it your team member, labor, supplier or partners. ❞**

To start with; we set up sales office at Mumbai. Currently we have sales offices in 6 countries including Honkong, US, Israel, Belgium, China and at 3 places in India (Kolkata, Bangalore, and Mumbai). We also are very aggressive in online sales and have customers from 152 countries. We have developed the dedicated team to work on it.

These are the major hurdles that we rectified and eliminated and that propelled our growth.

Current Status:

We are actively involved in the polished diamonds, jewellery manufacturing and marketing. Our last year gross revenue was approx. $ 800 million (approx. 5000 crore) and we are among top 5 in the industry in terms of manufacturing.

Key success factors:

There are several factors that contributed to our success and have made us what we are.

First and the most critical is 'Trust'. This industry mostly runs on trust. My father and Tulsi kaka always advised us that if you trust someone, trust fully. Be it your team member, labor, supplier or partners. If you have half trust, you will not delegate the responsibilities to them and thus, you will not get the best performance from all of them.

One aspect where we have been very strong and particular is our payments to vendors and suppliers. We have never made late payments ever.

Second is 'Taking calculative risk'. We have found that our founders were great risk takers. They started this business when they had nothing. They kept on taking a periodic risk and it is because of those risks' that we have reached till here. Even today when we are in the dilemma of whether

> **We have a culture where each person can raise their voice even on the policies of the company and can write directly to the MD.**

to take a particular decision or not, they encourage us to take calculated risks.

When we believe in ourselves and our experiences and take the risks, 8 out of 10 decisions are right.

Third is 'developing a great team'. The team plays a very crucial role in the success of any organization and thus we have certain practices in our organization. Our culture is such that we get the best out of our most of the people.

We have a flat organization and there is no difference in terms of treatment to people. Even we as owners mix with the team at the grass root level while they are working. At times, newcomers mistakenly identify us as fellow workers.

We have a culture where each person can raise their voice even on the policies of the company and can write directly to the MD.

We run a free of cost clinic for our team as well as people from surrounding area.

If a worker passes away we share amount between 2 lakhs to 10 lakh based on the need of the hour and the seniority of a person. For people who complete minimum 2 years in the company, we take their insurance for the financial security of their family. We take care of our people and always ensure that they are happy.

For the last 18 months there has been a recession in the diamond industry, yet we have not relieved a single person from the company. If we take care of them for few months, they will take care of us for many years to come.

Our team is one of the leading donors of blood in Surat. If we organize the blood donation camp, we collect 800 to 900 bottles of blood. We hold a very good reputation for this.

> *My father always told me to keep my eyes, ears and mind open so that whenever we visit other places or meet new people, we are able to learn from them through listening and observations.*

Our team is very powerful and committed and we are very happy about it.

The fourth factor is 'constant learning'. I always tell the youngsters to keep learning. We can learn from everyone, every event, anywhere and anytime.

My father always told me to keep my eyes, ears and mind open so that whenever we visit other places or meet new people, we are able to learn from them through listening and observations.

To promote learning culture, we have a dedicated library in our company. We focus on team training and development and conduct several developmental seminars in a year. We also have an in-house training center.

Social Contribution:

We are one of the leading contributors in the 500 bed hospital that is going to be developed for the benefit of all diamond industry workers. This hospital is equipped with air ambulance. 200 trustees from diamond industry has made the joint investments for this project. My father is head of the Patidar Saamaj, He also is one of the trustee in this hospital.

My father and Tulsibhai donated Surat Gurukul land, since they are the alumni of it. He also is one of the trustees for group of 40 gurukuls.

At gurukul they learnt lot of values and they had committed to do something for this institute and trust.

We are one of the donors for Saurashtra Jaldhara trust. Saurashtra had water crisis for long. Through this trust, more than 100 check dams were developed and as a result, today Saurashtra has enough water and the agricultural output has grown. This has created more prosperity in Saurashtra. esp. in rural areas.

> ❝ We are very proud and happy to inform you that we are the company that bought the Jodhpuri suit that our honorable prime minister wore on 26th January parade in 1st year of his office, for Rs. 4.31 crore. ❞

We also have adopted 2 govt. schools and are managing and ensuring its smooth operations.

MODI Suit:

We are very proud and happy to inform you that we are the company that bought the Jodhpuri suit that our honorable prime minister wore on 26th January parade in 1st year of his office, for Rs. 4.31 crore. That suit has been recently certified by Guinness Books as the most expensive suit of the world.

The rationale behind this step was little socio-religious. Over the last 15 years we regularly travel to Hrishikesh and have observed that Ganga river is getting dirtier and wanted to do something for it. And this suit was auctioned for that cause.

We are also actively involved in the Surat diamond hub development at khajod, Surat. GJEPC. We all leading players of diamond industry wanted a dedicated market for sales in Surat because the travelling and accommodation is very tough and at times very risky when people carry cash or diamonds with them for trading purpose.

This is much more difficult for people who don't have their own vehicles, for people who have small businesses and for people who are new into this industry. We all thought about it and decided to create a sales hub in Surat itself. This will bring all types of national and international buyers to Surat.

Future Road Map:

I think we still have a very long way to go. We all are still young and our sole focus is on the diamond business. We still desire to grow bigger in this business itself.

> **❝** *I am also very much inspired with the life of Warren buffet, he was a newspaper seller and today he is one of the richest person of the world and yet he has donated most of his wealth for the benefit of the larger society.* **❞**

Sales target is 1 billion $ in the next 5 years. Once we achieve this, we might think about diversification. I have often been fascinated by the software industry and might choose to opt for it in the near future.

When we came into business, we saw our parents do lot of hard work and we learnt the same from them. But our children are travelling in Mercedes and other expensive cars from their early childhood and they have a luxurious life so we can't expect them to do the same amount of hard work. Our next generation might come up with new business ideas and we will have to respect their wish.

We will send our next generation for effective business training and if at all, they want to join this business, they will have to go and work for some other company where professionalism is at its best and where they learn the values of discipline and dedication. Only then they should join our business.

My Heroes:

My role models from whom I have learnt meaningful lessons of life and business are; First and foremost, my father Mr. Lalji Patel, next is Dayal kaka, a stoic and placid person and Tulsi kaka.

Apart from this I have recently been very inspired with Satyanarayanji Goenka who was part of Vipasyana. He was an entrepreneur turned spiritual messenger. I have learnt a lot from him and also have done full 10 days Vipasyana process under his guidance.

I am also very much inspired with the life of Warren buffet, he was a newspaper seller and today he is one of the richest person of the world and yet he has donated most of his wealth for the benefit of the larger society.

My advice to other entrepreneurs is:

- Always Trust people and work with spirit of teamwork.
- Use technology to the fullest
- Never compromise on your values –Education should not make you arrogant, but should also teach you humility and values. Education without values is of no use.

FROM GOOD TO GREAT

Prafful ®

Mr. Narain Agrawal
Director

Firm Name
Prafful Sarees & Dress Materials

Estd: 1950

Products Or Services
Mfg. of Fashion Fabrics

For Mr. Narayan Agarwal, the decision to run the business came at the cost of compromising on his studies. Yet, he took it up gladly and has brought phenomenal success to the brand 'Prafful Sarees'. their host of other businesses of embroidery, dyeing and printing, manufacturing of nylon yarn, retail etc. has enabled them to secure turnovers as huge as 550 crores INR. With the entry of 2nd generation, this group is all set to take a next big leap.

Prafull Sarees

"There is no age for learning, if you are dedicated; there are multiple sources for learning on any subject in today's world."

.... *Narain Agarwal*

Mr. Narain Agrawal is the eldest brother among the 3 and is currently managing the group business as a key decision maker, of course with the full and unconditional support from his 2 brothers and of 5 children from 2nd generation.

He mentions that; Shri Satyanarayan Agarwal, my grandfather, started the business in our family in 1950.

My father was LLB and worked with Shreeram mills, but later joined the family business. We were the dealers for entire north India for Bombay mills and were mainly active in Kanpur and Delhi.

As time passed by, we did tie up with multiple manufacturers to increase turnover. The business was very good and we were making 8 to 10 lakhs profit per anum. Which was great in those days.

My younger brother Jaynarayan entered the family business, 2 years prior to me because I was interested in completing my B. Com. I wanted to study further and do CA but dropped on father's request.

When I entered in 1977, for first couple of years, I analyzed that we were over dependent on our suppliers, also that we were four people from

> ❝ We observed that traders were paying 2.5% interest rate per month for bill discounting and yet they were making good money, which means that business at Surat had good scope and healthy profitability. ❞

the family in the same business and needed better growth. Thus, I started searching for another business.

We started wholesale business of electrical goods at Bhagirath Palace, Delhi. It was a partnership business. After 3 years' partnership dissolved and I left that business to re-join the family business. But the search was still on for something better.

I realized that fabric trading is our strength so why not produce our own goods, applying backward integration strategy. The option in those days for fabric manufacturing were Mumbai, Ahmedabad or Surat.

Mumbai will be direct competition to our own suppliers so we cancelled that idea; Ahmedabad was a depressing market at that time. Surat seemed as a lucrative market because we observed that traders were paying 2.5% interest rate per month for bill discounting and yet they were making good money, which means that business had good scope and healthy profitability. We chose Surat and started our trading business.

Establishing Business at Surat:

We started with trading in 1987, at Surat Textile Market and dealt in sarees. In the next 3 years, we spread to three different markets in Surat itself.

This was good initial success for us.

The reason behind this success was hard work, delivering products that offer proper 'value for money', customer satisfaction and focus on quality. We always dealt with people who were famous for good quality, be it weavers or a process house etc.

Because of all this, we got good loyalty from our customers.

By 1990 we realized that we have good sales, thus we decided to do backward integration and started process house in 1992. After initial

> **When we invested in shifli, there were only 2 or 3 machines in entire Surat and there were only two manufacturers of shifli machines in the entire world.**

years of operations, we went for our first expansion in 1994–95 with 2 stanters, second expansion in 1997-98 with 4 stanters.

In 2000 we invested in embroidery work, and brought two Shifli machines. The cost of which was 2.5 crore per machine in those days. Today, we have 10 such machines and also have 48 multiheads machines.

When we invested in Shifli, there were only 2 or 3 machines in entire Surat and there were only two manufacturers of Shifli machines in the world. I had advance anticipation of market trends and knew that this will be a successful investment. I always had a thought that we should be ahead of change and grab new opportunities before others do.

It was a calculated risk, as we already had work on hand. We used to get it done from Delhi and thought, why not, do it for self.

We had gross turnover of Rs. 40 crores and we went on to invest 5 crores in these machines, which was a substantial capital, and huge risk in those days. But as it is said that entrepreneurship is all about taking calculated risk. At times not taking a risk is a bigger risk.

After this we were recognized by the market as trendsetters. We always wanted to be the leader and not the follower.

Currently we have full value chain except weaving, because that segment had over production capacity in Surat. After all, why should we invest in weaving machines when we get the product at good rates, as per our specifications and whenever we wanted.

Expansion:

Once all the businesses were settled, I anticipated that more kids from family will enter the business and we will need more businesses in the group. So we decided to enter in nylon threads manufacturing.

There were lot of thread manufacturing companies in market, but only few players produced nylon thread so it seemed as a good option.

> *Because of all these developments and timely decisions, we have grown 10 times in last 15 years.*

Those days' polyester thread was a competitive price market with lot of big players already into action, including Reliance.

We first started production of nylon thread in 2009. Initially with 200 tons per month, later scaled its capacity to 400 tons and now 800 tons. Expansion work is in progress to further scale the production capacity to 1400 tons per month.

Our quality was excellent and that is the reason behind its rapid expansion.

No one in the family had any knowhow about nylon manufacturing but we were open to new learnings and that made all the difference.

There is no age for learning, if you are dedicated; there are multiple sources for learning on any subject in today's world.

I had always focused on constant learning and upgrading myself. I got deeper into enhancing my knowledge about the subject. And I am happy that we could execute the project successfully.

It was a major risk, but family supported us. It was a big leap for us. But again it was a calculated risk. My brothers always respected me and my decisions. We all are eager to grow and work hard.

Because of all these developments and timely decisions, we have grown 10 times in last 15 years.

I also want to mention that we are very thankful to State Bank of India. They are our bankers and have stood by us and have provided timely funds as per the need of the business, without which the rapid growth would have not been achieved.

Current status:

We 3 brothers are managing the entire group business with the excellent support and involvement of our next generation. Myself Narian Agarwal, younger brothers; Jay Narayan Agarwal and Pankaj Agarwal who is 9 years younger to me.

> *Jab kuchh nahi hota hai tab unity zyada hoti hai. Par jab kuchh hota hai toh disputes bhi hote hai. Hum is mamle me khusnaseeb hai.*

My elder son Raveesh manages the nylon thread manufacturing unit at Panoli, Gujarat. Younger son Varun manages the retail business, both online and offline. He is also currently working on a new business venture, which we might launch very soon.

Prafful, son of Jay Narayan is active with his father at our process house and Aayush, son of Pankaj has recently joined after completion of his MBA and is currently under my coaching and very soon he will be on his independent role.

Currently we have manufacturing and trading of suits, sarees and kurtis. We have our own dying and printing unit, embroidery unit, and retail operations with 150+ SIS at all leading lifestyle retailing stores of modern trade.

We also have significant presence in online retail, & the last in the list is nylon thread manufacturing which is the major contributor in our gross revenues. Our last year cumulative gross annual revenues were approx. Rs. 550 Crore.

All the businesses operate as independent entities. We don't interfere in day-to-day workings of others' territory, assuming that he knows what is right.

We are further expanding our nylon thread production capacity this year. And we are also about to launch a new diversified business venture under the leadership of Varun.

Current Challenges:

"Jab kuchh nahi hota hai tab unity zyada hoti hai. Par jab kuchh hota hai toh disputes bhi hote hai. Hum is mamle me khusnaseeb hai". [When there is nothing, the bonding and unity is strong. But it is very hard to maintain the same bonding once you have something. We have been fortunate in this matter].

> ❝ before spending on marketing or branding we must have a clear back up plan for scaling and expansion or else there is no point spending money behind marketing. ❞

Generation gap is the considerable challenge and to manage this effectively, we have a simple but very effective strategy. We have placed all our children under the leadership of uncles and not the fathers and also they are rotated on diff. businesses under the leadership of diff. person. This way, they get to learn about each business within the group and they learn to deal with different people.

Key learnings through business:

There are certain learnings that we have derived from the entire experience of several years. To mention few of them:

First is related to marketing. 'Prafful' is a good consumer brand and well recognized by end users. We invested a lot on television advertisement with ZEE TV between the years 1994 to 1997. Thus, we are still recognized, even today as a good brand. Honestly speaking we popularized the brand but could not encash it through right sales volume.

Learning we derived from this was: before spending on marketing or branding we must have a clear back up plan for scaling and expansion or else there is no point spending money behind marketing.

Second learning is related to 'problem solving'. We have spent so many years into the business that these days' problems don't seem like problem, they seem like routine issue.

"Problems toh roz hi aate hai aur bahot aate hai, but yeh depend karta hai ki aap kitna oon par concentrate karte hai, aap kitna uske bare me sochte hai. Problems ko zyada mind space nahi dena chaiye – problem se daroge toh aage kaise badhoge." [Problems are necessary part of business but it largely depends upon your approach and on how much mind space do you allot to them. We should not overthink about them. If you are afraid of problems, you can't grow]

Third learning is related to the 'quality'.

> **" We want to cross the 1000 crore revenue per annum by 2020. "**

Good quality can't be delivered just by having good thoughts; we need to take concrete steps for it. One needs best quality materials, suppliers, QC process, your people should also be of great quality, and all this does not come at cheaper rates. But we did not focus on profitability; rather we accepted whatever rates market was willing to offer and tried to give best possible quality in those rates.

Fourth learning is related to 'future vision'.

Till date we had never thought about future targets or vision. But now we all the family members are involved into professional trainings on business management and leadership, and have realized the power of a clear vision and thus, each respective business leader has developed a clear vision for self. We want to cross the 1000 crore revenue per annum by 2020.

Fifth learning is related to our 'Team'. Team plays a very critical role in successful running of any venture and that is why, we have always focused on developing loyalty in teams and are successful in maintaining 90% team members from day one.

For our Teams, we have always taken care of their needs, we invest in their regular trainings, we offer food at subsidized rates within factory premise. Transportation facilities were provided so that they can comfortably work, we celebrate all festivals so that they get comfortable with the other team members and have homely feel.

Key regrets:

Key mistakes that I regret are; we could not encash on our brand building activities and investments.

Next is, I always wanted all our kids to get more educated, which did not happen with some of them. Today's market is more complex and competitive and it needs better knowledge and responses. And for that, I think they should have been better qualified

> ❝ *Today, everyone is qualified. But making yourself superior among all the qualified people is a major challenge, and only those who could do it, will be the leaders of tomorrow.* ❞

We are currently focused more on preparing our next generation so that they can successfully take this group to greater heights in future. For that, we have enrolled them into entrepreneurial and managerial training programs and we are coaching them under first generation leaders.

Future plans are that each family member must have their own independent business or venture.

Learning is important:

Constant learning has been the trump card for us, even about the subjects on which we had no idea, but was necessary for running the business. I was 50 when I thought about nylon thread manufacturing, and went on to a long journey for learning about it, spent lot of time and travelled to multiple countries to develop necessary clarity and knowledge.

Today, everyone is qualified. But making yourself superior among all the qualified people is a major challenge, and only those who could do it, will be the leaders of tomorrow.

With the help of constant learning, we stayed ahead of market and were trendsetters. We entered into businesses ahead of time or at the development stage instead of maturity stage.

Our Social Contribution activities are many:

We have been always involved in religious activities and social work, it is a legacy of our father. We are active donor to poor and needy families and for donating in dharamshala development. Since Last 12 years, I am very active in Agarwal samaj and was president for couple of years.

Working for community upgradation and encouraging community people for social service is my major focus area.

> ❝ *In business some days are good and some are bad, but at the end of the day, you forget everything when you are with your family. It gives you inner peace* ❞

Health and education are the two areas that attract me more and I keenly work for initiatives related to it.

I am the trustee in a school 'Agarwal Vidya Vihar', 3000 student study over there. Availing qualitative education at one-third fees.

I am one of the trustees of cancer hospital in civil campus, Trustee in charitable hospital where we treat at subsidized rates to needy people, I am part of different trade councils related to yarn and exports promotions. Also the part of Surat marathon organizing committee' for Surat municipal corporation as a director.

Trustee for traffic education committee, CCTV camera installation committee (for which all the funds has been raised from Pvt. Sector), traffic brigade management committee which operates on PPP model.

In coming years, I want to spend my 50% time for social activities. Which at present is 20%.

Role of family in our success:

I would just say that, the real happiness in life can come only through family. In business some days are good and some are bad, but at the end of the day, you forget everything when you are with your family. It gives you inner peace.

My sources of Inspiration:

I have no role models as such but I learn from anyone in whom I see good qualities. Different people have different qualities to learn from.

I admire Jayanti bhai kabutarwala from Colourtex.

His style of running a business and management is best, I have learnt a lot from him.

I also learn by meeting better people and by being in company of good and learned people. But the big differentiator is that I also quickly implement what I learn.

My advice to young entrepreneurs is:

- Success is not a lottery; you must earn it. Success without efforts is tasteless. So don't look for shortcuts or ride on other people's efforts. Do it for yourself and you will value the success and really enjoy it.

- Traditional thinking will not work. We need to modernize our thinking and look forward, and also prepare ourselves in advance. In olden days, less capable or lesser IQ guys could also create a good business, but it is not possible today. So prepare yourself very well.

THE MATTERS OF THE HEART

Mr. Bhargav Kotadia
Executive Director

Firm Name:
Sahajanand Technologies Pvt. Ltd.

Estd:1993

Products or Services
Technological Solutions for Diamond & Health Care Industries

Mr. Dhirajlal Kotadia had established the firm from an extremely modest background. From a seller of miscellaneous goods on trains, he founded the company as a provider of technological solutions to textile and diamond industry. His son Mr. Bhargav Kotadia's involvement in the business has brought in greater R&D initiatives and it's commercialization and thus Shahajanand group has grown into the predominant producer of heart stents, laser machines for diamond cutting and polishing, Ayurvedic medicines etc. housing the turnover of nearly 200 crores INR.

Sahajanand Technologies Pvt. Ltd.

"We always focus on; how can we bring the benefits of advanced technologies to the masses?"

...... Bhargav Kotadia

Mr. Bhargav Kotadia narrates how his father, Mr. Dhirajlal Kotadia founded the company in late 80's.

He moved to Surat from Chennai, because at that time Surat was assumed and known to be the fastest growing cities of India and offered several growth opportunities.

He started the business with solar cell, popularly known as wafer; a small component for textile looms machine. The initial business took off and we settled here.

My father was always an entrepreneur and had an habit to save and then would invest those savings into some or the other business idea or product.

Back in Chennai he was selling pens and pencils on trains, yet he managed to save some money and invested it into gas and lighter agency. Grew that business and gave it to someone and he moved to Surat.

My father was very technically adept person and also had a skill set, foresight and a vision to see what will be the future 10 or 20 years later.

> **❝ If manpower is limited and you rely heavily on them for productivity, your growth will also be limited. ❞**

This comes from his basic understanding about fundamentals of physics and engineering. There are plenty of engineers outside but very few out of them are strong at fundamentals of engineering and my father was one of them who can understand the things to the very core and how to apply it to solve practical problems with the help of particular technology.

He was a diploma holder in Electronics & Sound technology and had 6 months' internship experience from ECI [Electric Corporation of India], Hyderabad. Where he was working on laser sound technology. This was his first encounter with laser technology.

Initial years at Surat:

When he came to Surat, which was known for its textile and diamond industry, his constant thought was 'how his knowledge can help the industry to grow and be more profitable?'

Here he observed that diamond industry was growing very fast but it was heavily labor intensive. The diamond cutting to polishing time was taking more than a month. Since people in Surat were largely into job work, due to slow, manual and labor dependent process, the productivity and the earning capacity of the entire industry was limited.

If manpower is limited and you rely heavily on them for productivity, your growth will also be limited.

Around same time, laser technology was developed in some part of the world. My dad came across the information about that technology. It was a lab grown Swiss company, which provided this technology but it was very expensive.

My dad went to an exhibition in Germany, and that is where he saw for the first time the laser technology and thought about bringing that technology to India and solve several problems of local industry.

> ❝ *We wrote on each of our machines in bold letters 'Proudly Made in India'* ❞

He convinced one of the diamond polishing company owner to invest in the R&D of laser machine for diamond cutting. They bought the machines from the Swiss company and used it for diamond cutting. Once convinced with the performance, they opened the machine for the purpose of learning and did reverse engineering on it and created a local version of that machine at much cheaper cost. The R&D took almost 3 years.

This machine helped people to cut the diamond within 24hours, which earlier used to take full month. It was a great overnight success and that helped us establish this company. We sold those machines in large numbers and for almost 15 years, we had no competition at all.

We are very proud of this achievement. We wrote on each of our machines in bold letters **'Proudly Made in India'**

Later on we sourced other technologies for diamond industry. We also had worked with Sarin for almost 6 years. Sarin had developed the technology for diamond planning which helped people to plan the shape and size of diamonds and gain better productivity.

Launching Medical Technology Business:

Once we achieved the market leadership, we entered into heart stent manufacturing business. In those days, few American companies were producing it but selling it at prohibitive cost, completely out of reach of a common man. The cost of each stent was 5 to 6 lakh Indian rupees and that excluded the surgery cost.

The technology to produce heart stent was again laser. We realized that we can do it much more efficiently; we can do it at much cheaper cost and yet deliver the same quality that the American guys were delivering to the market.

> **"America has some of the best technologies, but unless we bring the cost of those technologies down, it will not help the world."**

Our entry into the heart stent manufacturing business and establishment of Sahajanand Medical Technologies Pvt. Ltd. was due to an incident that shook my dad.

Once my dad went to a medical store for buying some medicines where he saw an old man crying because he needed some medicine for his dear one, but he did not had enough money. My dad instantly paid for him but he was shaken from within.

He could not sleep for whole night and thought that this kind of incidents might be happening every day and at several drug stores. Do I have enough money to help all of them? Even if I have all the money, can I go and stand at each store and help people? The answer for both the question was 'No'.

That is when he decided to create a medical technology company that can reduce the cost of health care. Probably that was the only way we could have helped millions of people.

We always focus on; how can we bring the benefits of advanced technologies to the masses?

Our approach is very clear, we pick a technology and look at what people are doing with it? Then we ask about, can we do it better? Can we do it cheaper? and Can we make it affordable for the masses? Because if we do the same as what others are doing, there is no point.

America has some of the best technologies, but unless we bring the cost of those technologies down, it will not help the world.

From an 100% import dependent country, we are proud to inform that India has become one of the leading exporter of heart stent to world market. Sahajanand itself exports to more than 50 countries including most part of the Europe.

In 2001, we ventured into herbal food supplements and Ayurvedic medicines.

> **❝** *Ayurveda has solutions to most of our diseases and problems but we never look at it as one of the legitimate solution* **❞**

My father realized that at the end of the day, whatever we do, solves only one particular problem. For an example the stent solves cardiac problem but what about other parts of the body? What can we do for full body cure?

Pharma industry, then and even now, has certain issues. There is a very long and tedious process for new drug development. It takes 6 to 7 years to bring any new product to the market. From development to clinical trial to regulatory, and even after doing all this, there are always some side effects of the chemical used in the medicine.

Any medicine at the end of the day is chemical and since chemical is a foreign material for the body; our body does not accept it. It creates some or the other kind of reaction in the body. No medicine or chemical is without reaction.

For an example; any medicine for arthritis has chemicals that are very toxic and has severe side effects, and one such side effect is, it causes cardiac disease. The worst part is, these medicines are mostly consumed by the senior citizens.

We realized that Ayurveda has solutions to most of our diseases and problems but we never look at it as one of the legitimate solution. It is always there, present in every Indian kitchen.

Avg. Americans spend 10 times more money on health care than Indians, why is that? It is because they heavily rely on chemical for every cure. On the contrary, every single ingredient in our Indian kitchen is medicine. Right from spices and herbs that we use in our cooking. Our food design created by our forefathers has medicine properties imbibed within.

We thought; can we bring this solution to the masses? We also knew that it wouldn't work with Ayurveda name on it. We had to give it a new form and a new name to develop a completely new perception about it in the mind of end user.

> **"** Our mission focus is on: How can we bring solutions and technologies that are into the hands of select few and pass the benefits of it on to the masses? Where it actually has a bigger impact. **"**

We did R&D on it for almost 10 years, both; in India as well as in US. We have a big lab in USA, with some of the best doctors and scientist working on this project. Just about 3 years back we launched the prescription based products under the brand name of 'Pink Health' through doctors.

6 months back we launched direct to consumer product under the name of 'Su-Aayu', it is for arthritis and joint aids. Shortly we are coming up with diagnostic devices.

Current status:

Presently we are into the business of Laser cutting machines for diamond industry, heart stent and herbal food supplements.

We also are investing in lot many other businesses that we find in sync with our ideology.

Approx. 700 people are working for us with gross 200cr annual business.

Our mission focus is on: How can we bring solutions and technologies that are into the hands of select few and pass the benefits of it on to the masses? Where it actually has a bigger impact.

Jugadu innovations in laser diamond cutting machines reduced the cost of technology and also helped our industry to improve its productivity and achieve greater scale.

Same is with stent, the stent that was available at 5 to 6 lakhs was launched by us at 1.5 lakh rupees. Which now is available at much cheaper cost. Today the starting price is 25k. And this is exactly what we intended to do.

We always wanted to enter any industry to bring its cost down and not to take it up. This was against the conventional thought of industry, which focus on making higher profits in shortest possible time.

> **While engineers, doctors and scientists create new products and solutions, my role is to convert these new developments into a viable business models**

We think exactly opposite. Much on the lines of what Henry Ford thought and did in automobile industry. He brought the benefits of technology to the masses. If few people used cars, it will not help the industry as well as the economy. If some companies had trucks, it will not help. But if it is used by masses, it greatly impacts the economy and the world.

My father is not an official engineer [he is a diploma holder], but he is one of the best engineer, scientist and even a doctor that I know. Because whatever education he had, he always focused on fundamental understanding about whatever subject he learnt. He never insisted us for better grades; he always encouraged us to develop better understanding about whatever we learn. Our parents never asked us or forced us for better grades.

My Involvement is Business:

I am into this business since 2011. First year, I was in US and worked for our diet supplementary project. In 2012, I returned to India. Dec 2013, I started working for this company over here.

We are 3 siblings. I have a degree in economics. By qualification I am an economist and thus, I am passionately interested in finance, esp. in corporate finance.

So, while engineers, doctors and scientists create new products and solutions, my role is to convert these new developments into a viable business models, adding the commercial aspect to it. I am more into commercial aspect of our business.

Future plans

Looking ahead in future I think our medical technology business will grow faster, the other two businesses are kind of mature. In stent, we are one of

> *Apple outsourced mobile phone manufacturing, in spite of their own capabilities. They focused only on developing new products through R&D. this is called specialization.*

the fastest growing in the industry. Just 3 years back, we were at 35 cr., this year it would be 100cr, next year we might be crossing 200 crores.

Our vision is to develop a public limited company having 2500 to 3000 crores annual revenue.

For Stent Company, going public will be within 5 to 6 years. For diet supplement business, the timeline is not clear.

At present the focus is on organizing the current business and bring professional management system. We are also investing heavily in technologies that help us to manage better.

In future, we want to invest into lot many businesses as a parent company and operate as a conglomerate.

We will have capital, business acumen, the systems and leadership capabilities. We will invest all this in multiple businesses and do macro managing. Each business will have their own separate leadership and management team so that they can focus on their individual businesses.

Focus and Specialization

I believe focus and specialization is must in 21st century. Apple outsourced mobile phone manufacturing, in spite of their own capabilities. They focused only on developing new products through R&D. this is called specialization.

We will search for people who have great products, ideas or solutions and invest in their ventures. People who have very good products and solutions to offer to the masses. We want to create a long-lasting organization.

My Current Role:

I am good at two things; finance and strategic investments.

> **We were the first in the world to develop Bio degradable polymer used in heart stent**

What to invest, when to invest, at what rate & In what products and services? Is my forte.

In each industry, along with few good companies, there are many others who are profit minded. Each business has competition, there are many who don't want you to survive or grow because you are disrupting their markets and profit structure. And my role is to see that we not only survive against such competitive forces but also excel in whatever we do.

The individual entrepreneurs leading each business unit will take care of products & solutions and they will also take great care of their respective customers.

Present day challenges:

The biggest issue we faced till date in business is related to people. How to attract and retain good people in the organization?

When we don't get the right people at the right time, we have to hire people with lesser abilities and somehow learn to manage them and get the best performance from them.

Even today if we want to hire good scientists, doctors, engineers or managers and ask them to come to Surat, leaving metro cities, they don't come. So now we are in process to set up our R&D in some other city.

Learning from our mistakes

We had few very powerful learning's through our business, which has made us little wise. Some of the major learning's came from our own mistakes and ignorance.

One of the costliest mistakes we made was due to lack of right knowledge. We did not know anything about IPR's and patents.

> **One of the strongest ability of my dad was to identify the right people and groom them into great resource.**

We were the first in the world to develop Bio degradable polymer used in heart stent, but were not very keen on commercial aspect of it. Hence, we did not filed for patents and unknowingly we made it open to people. One of the American companies came to us, showed interest in working with us [at least they gave that impression], they learnt from us about the technology and they filed for patent in their name.

Had we known about patents at that point of time, today our that company alone would have had INR 1000 crore turnover. Small mistake – big cost.

Teams role in our success

My father started without much capital, did lot of hard work and created a company, though he was all alone. I guess he was able to do it largely because of people, dedicated loyal people who worked hand in hand with him. They put every ounce of their blood and sweat into the development of this organization. Even in the R&D and all the innovations. It was a dedicated effort by the team of engineers.

One of the strongest ability of my dad was to identify the right people and groom them into great resource. Many of them are with us today and are heading some of our group businesses. Some of them who left and are working with other companies or are running their own businesses are in top leadership position or are leaders of their industry. And we are very satisfied about this fact.

Today almost half a dozen laser machine manufacturers and half a dozen stent manufacturers are operating in this market and almost all of them can trace their roots to Sahajanand. Such was the grooming of dad with people.

He taught them about products, about the management, about how to do the business, how to manage finances and how to interact with outside

> **Tata does everything under the sun and they are $100 billion company, Apple does only one thing with great focus and they are $ 700-billion company.**

companies. He taught all this in a manner that, they can implement all those learning's successfully in their lives. For us this is one of our winning points. This is what we always wanted, more people working towards bringing benefits of technology to common man.

Our key success factors:

They are many; but 'Focus' is one of the major reasons. It is easy to get de-focused and very hard to stay focused. Focus is the hardest thing to do. This is one of the major problems with Indian companies; they are guiltier for this than anyone else.

Look at apple, they had all the opportunity to get into various business but they never lost their focus and are committed to R & D and bring awesome digital gadgets to the market.

We also had lot many such opportunities to do everything under the sun, but we always thought about few basics; What we are good at? what we can be good at? And what are the needs of customers and markets? Think only about your target customer, don't think about all the customers of all the companies. If you design for everyone, you will end up designing for no one.

Tata does everything under the sun and they are $100 billion company, Apple does only one thing with great focus and they are $ 700-billion company. Microsoft makes one thing; they are $ 400-billion company. Google doing one thing $ 500-billion company.

I had visited a company near Baroda, Gujarat. They had their manufacturing unit. Right next to it, there was a resort which they had built just because they had lot of visitors who need a good accommodation facility. Then they had a separate marketing company which did marketing only for them. I said are you people crazy? Ask some good hotel company to come and put up a hotel next door they are good at hotel management, not you. Ask an advertising and marketing

> *Give away couple of lakh rupees' extra salary if the guy is good, because in the longer run, that same guy, after 5 to 7 years would be your greatest strength and resource, and will prove much cheaper. To accept this is esp. more challenging in family managed businesses. Please avoid nepotism (Hiring relatives instead of qualified professionals)*

company to do marketing for you; they will do it for few lakh rupees so that you can focus on your core business. And they will do it cheaper and better than you.

This is why American companies are American companies and why Indian companies are Indian companies.

In Sahajanand, one point of time, even we were committing the same mistake; we had a software company, we had a marketing company, we had a laser machine manufacturing company, we had a hotel company etc. I asked them to stop all those businesses and focus on one or two things at which we are better than anyone else.

Always focus and try not to deviate.

Along with focus, 'Timing' is another critical element. When you launch a product, service or initiative, the timing has to be right. For UBER, the timing was just right, if they had been early, they must have gone bankrupt.

Same is with 'Air BNB'. After 2008 crisis, people were open to an idea about a stranger staying in their house, and thus, they succeeded. Had this concept been launched two or three years earlier, it would have been a failure.

The third factor that I feel is important for our success and for any other company is, Hire right people. This is very critical. Hence, spend as much time as you can on hiring and have patience.

Give away couple of lakh rupees' extra salary if the guy is good, because in the longer run, that same guy, after 5 to 7 years would be your greatest strength and resource, and will prove much cheaper. To accept this is esp. more challenging in family managed businesses. Please avoid nepotism (Hiring relatives instead of qualified professionals)

My role in this company is to bring that discipline and focus & maintain this through out.

> *I do business because I love strategy, I love finance, I love competition, I love marketing and admire the solutions that businesses deliver to the masses*

Social Contribution:

We are very active in social contribution. All our social contribution goes through gurukul. 10% of our annual income goes to them because my father had studied in gurukul at Rajkot and he is very much attached to it.

Even in the matter of social contribution, we think, if Gurukul can do it better, cheaper and much more effectively than us, let them do it. We will just pass on the money to them.

Purpose of doing business:

If you are doing business for money and raising kids, this is the bad idea. You should not get into business for this reason.

I do business because I love strategy, I love finance, I love competition, I love marketing and admire the solutions that businesses deliver to the masses. I do it for the sheer joy of giving. Almost all the successful entrepreneurs are the ones who were passionate for something beyond money.

If you are doing business for money, even if you are successful, your life is miserable. These people are very stressed at the end of the day and you can figure out that these guys do not like what they are doing.

I do it for all the results that business produces. I have passion for products and I have passion for satisfying customers.

Importance of learning in life:

For both, my father and me the major source of learning has been reading and experiments.

My father since childhood is fond of reading. While he was in his fourth grade, he had read almost all books available in their school library and

> **❝** *Mahatma Gandhi lived and awesome life, he knew exactly what 4 to 5 things were necessary for his living, he just kept that and left the rest.* **❞**

that is why he is so stronger and better than any engineer who has degree but lesser understanding.

For me it is the same but with little difference. I read a lot about the world of finance and investments. I started reading and learning about it since I was 14 years old. Now, I focus more on strategy. I spend approx. 4 to 5 hours a day to learn new things and upgrade myself.

I learn a lot about what other companies are doing? What are their key strengths and weaknesses? How do they capture market, beat competition, gain market share, how they use technology in their business? etc. and that is the only sure way to grow and succeed in today's time?

My source of Inspiration:

For me my first role model is my father. His core ideas about business fundamentals on which he started coaching me since I was of 10 years old are the base of my understanding about the business.

Apart from him there are lot of business leaders, entrepreneurs and experts. I look at them and search for what they can offer me as learning.

I like Warren buffet for his financial ideas and concepts. His modest lifestyle really inspires me. It's one thing to have lot of money and it is very different to live a wonderful and fulfilling life.

Even mahatma Gandhi lived an awesome life, he knew exactly what 4 to 5 things were necessary for his living, he just kept that and left the rest.

Money can easily corrupt you and get you in the rat race of expensive bungalows and cars. To which, there is no end. But the same money can be spent for schools, for developing hospitals, for better health care, for housing and many such causes.

> **They say 'education is a master switch and a solution to several problems."**

There is a saying that 'there is enough in this world to fulfill the basic needs of every human, but there is not enough to satisfy the wants of a single person'. Wants never end, if allowed, most of the people want to rule the world and have everything that world has to offer.

Our education today is based on ratta, copy and paste from navneet guide. Our teachers too are so immature that even if you do a small grammar mistake in writing, they will mark the entire answer as incorrect, which is insane.

The true education to me is having lot of curiosity. Curiosity about why things work the way they work, why does a building stand straight and does not fall? Why does the phone work the way it works? Why a machine performs the way it performs? Why does my car work the way it works? Why does the sun shine on us every day? Why a person behaves the way he/she behaves? etc., this is true education for me.

Education is so very important that most of the leaders of today, work for this. Bill and Malinda gates foundation work for several issues, but primary of them is education.

They say 'education is a master switch and a solution to several problems. Once you educate people, they will solve many problems on their own'.

Following the same footsteps, I will not give money as a help to anyone but I will do everything to educate him/her. Education will empower him to not only feed himself for lifetime, but also he can take care of 10 more people. Teach fishing is what is more important.

My dad is a religious man and each human who lives with right values inspires him. He is inspired by several industrialists from Surat and elsewhere who have lot of money but they live a simple life themselves, and they also contribute a lot to the society.

> **The best part with India is that, we are getting wealth along with all the best learning's from others and thus we are not going to repeat those mistakes.**

In America and in large part of the west, first they earned a lot, they became spendthrift and got nothing from life. Finally they realized that helping others and living a simple life is the better way. Now you have the gates and the buffets to initiate this process.

The best part with India is that, we don't have to make those silly mistakes to learn from. We are getting wealth along with all the best learning's from others and thus we are not going to repeat those mistakes. We first know where and how to use the wealth and then we are getting a lot of it.

When I look towards future and think about the legacy that we want to leave behind. I think Sahajanand will be the core legacy we leave behind.

During my lifetime it will be on a global scale. We took it from local and are marching towards global presence. We will develop it as a global entity and leave it for future leaders to carry forward.

My advice to other entrepreneurs and esp. for young aspiring ones are:

- Never work for money, rather work with lot of passion and look for the opportunities to solve most pressing problem of the society.
- Search for opportunities to bring the benefits of the most advance technologies to the masses
- Learn a lot and always stay updated with latest developments of the world
- Share your fruits with the society, if you earn lot of money, use it wisely for the betterment of the society

Advice from Mr. Dhirajlal Kotadia:

- Never be afraid of hurdles and challenges, in fact each unsolved problem of society is a new business opportunity. If you can take up a problem and develop solution for it, same hurdle will become the base for creating a big business empire for you.

THE TASTE OF THE THIRST

Since 1923
Hajoori

Mr. Abbas Hajoori
Director Partner

Firm Name:
Hajoori & Sons

Estd: 1923

Products or Services
Mfg. of Soft Drinks 'SOSYO' & Other Beverages

Mr. Abbas Hajoori had to grapple with the threats from multinational giants like Coke and Pepsi and carve out their own niche in the market. As a second generation entrepreneur the responsibility of carrying forward the brand 'SOSYO' and its business successfully was a rather tough one. However, not only did he excelled in all such expectations but also ushered a 100 crores INR turnover for the company, thus securing its brand value in the market.

SOSYO

"We don't focus on competition from Coke or Pepsi, We have a niche. Thus, we focus only on our products and our markets and try to deliver the best quality and taste."

.... *Abbas Hajoori*

This enterprise was initiated by his uncle Mr. Abbas Abdul Rahim Hajoori, informs Mr. Abbas Hajoori, the current owner of this business. Unfortunately, the family got wiped out due to communal riots. It was then that the business came to his father, Mr. Mohsin Hajoori. Mr. Abbas was a young boy at that time. He brought lot of changes in the business since the time he had joined.

My father was a staunch gandhian and always wore khadi. When the swadeshi movement started, we were buying flavors from WIMTO, a British company and were manufacturing as their franchisee. But my father being a true gandhian, decided to stop buying flavors from a British company and he developed lot of innovative flavors in house and also ventured into ice creams.

My initial years in business:

Eventually my elder brother entered the business and after few years, I joined the business. But we could not expand beyond a certain level because of ineffective management.

> **This journey has been full of struggle, learning and excitement.**

We managed the business with whatever limited knowledge we had and in the process, we missed an opportunity to create a bigger business. Coke and Pepsi have been in India since 1990. Parle and Dukes were the only other strong soft drink brands available in the Indian market those days. We now realize that we indeed had a great opportunity to create a strong Indian soft drink brand prior to the entry of multinationals. Sometimes, I regret the opportunities lost.

This journey has been full of struggle, learning and excitement.

When for the first time my brother sent me for marketing to Ahmedabad on the highway along with the truck, although the market for cold drinks was good, we could sell only 3 crates in total. But due to our perseverance, hard work and consistency of visits, the scenario changed and within a year we were selling approximately 300 crates in every trip.

A similar incident unfolded in Dumas, Surat. I realized that some of the retailers were selling cold drinks in large numbers. So I went to that market and persuaded one of the retailers to sell our products and obtained the orders of 6 crates. Next day that person came searching for us. We gave that retailer an icebox for storage and he purchased 30 crates.

We also had to hear, "I don't want your products and next time don't ever come to my place" from different people on different occasions. But I kept on visiting those retailers and after a year; many of them started dealing with us and are doing business with us even today.

All these experiences taught us a lot about marketing, sales and customer's psychology. We learnt to deal with difficult people and also learnt the art of convincing people to get the desired results.

Around 1997-98, the cold drink market in India went down by almost 40% while on the other hand, the multinationals were spending wildly in marketing to snatch the remaining business from the Indian operators as they came with huge marketing budget.

> ❝ *The soft drinks contain calcium carbonate, which works as an antiseptic on germs in our body and helps us to kill the germs. ENO is based on the same formula.* ❞

During the same period, several new local brands and companies also entered the soft drink business. We were attacked from both sides and this shook us for a while. We sat with the team and identified the problem. Mainly two major areas were identified as a scope of improvement. And those were; our pricing was little high and our packaging was old.

We changed our pricing and modernized our packaging, As a result we could overcome the bottlenecks and regain our market share.

Soft drinks are good for health:

One of the consistent challenges we faced and are still facing is market and consumer's perception that soft drinks are bad for health. To which I always reply, why don't we think that soft drinks are good? Actually they are good for our health.

Microbiological germs are not visible with naked eyes. When we get hurt or a cut, we apply antiseptic on it to prevent the damage. When we eat, we intake a lot of oral germs, then why don't we drink antiseptic after food?

The soft drinks contain calcium carbonate, which works as an antiseptic on germs in our body and helps us to kill the germs. ENO is based on the same formula.

For that matter, what is Indian tonic water?

It contains 'Quinine', the medicine for malaria, 'Water' to balance dehydration and 'Sugar' to pep up the energy. These are the same components for most of our drinks.

Whenever I get an opportunity to speak in public, I share this information with the people so that I can change their perception in however small capacity that may be.

After the sad demise of my father, there was a split among brothers over property rights. As a viable solution I kept the business and my

> **The last 5 years have been of good growth for us, due to fresh ideas and zeal bought by my son.**

brothers kept the properties and assets and went on to create their respective businesses

This is a common problem in many family businesses, initially it is one leader. Usually, a father with many sons working under him, but once he is out, who will lead, Becomes the big question. Since there is no clear leader in the 2nd or the 3rd generation, most businesses collapse.

According to me, in any family business, few characteristics must be very strong.

First, there should be single leader or authority. Second, the understanding among the members of the family must be good. Third, each person from the family must be working and no one should be idle and finally. Fourth, the business should be big enough to split so that each one has a sizeable pie in their share.

Although my brothers denied running the business, I had visualized a different future and had also anticipated the worth of the 'SOSYO' brand. And thus kept it with me and worked very hard to further develop this brand. Today I am happy that I had made that decision.

Entry of 3rd generation:

My son entered this business 5 years back, after completing his M-Com. "I am the 2nd generation entrepreneur and my son is the 3rd generation." The last 5 years have been of good growth for us, due to fresh ideas and zeal bought by my son.

Apart from the four people in the top management, we have relatively young team and the younger generation doesn't like to sit idle.

Current status:

Today we have INR 100 crore plus revenue per annum, having bottling plants at 15 locations, spread across five states of India; Gujarat, Maharashtra, MP, Chhattisgarh and Rajasthan.

> ❝ We solved the funding problem by applying the OPM (other people's money) principle and thought that franchising can be a good option ❞

There are various international operations in the pipeline. We are putting up manufacturing facility at Lusaka and Zambia, the operations will start very soon over there.

One out of the fifteen locations is our own manufacturing unit and the remaining 14 are franchisees. Our franchisees handle both; the manufacturing as well as sales.

Franchising has worked for us:

The idea to create such franchisee model was developed out of necessity.

We wanted to expand and grow faster but we didn't have the necessary money and needed external funds. Since we don't believe in paying or charging interest on capital, the bank funding option was not the viable idea for us. We solved that problem by applying the OPM (other people's money) principle and thought that franchising can be a good option where the franchisees will invest in the production capacity, in logistics and in transportation for market supply.

This model has worked very well for us. It brings funds for expansion of manufacturing facility, it brings the necessary focus on a territory as the franchisees work very hard for their ROI and above all, it brings ownership of investing entrepreneurs who work with a greater sense of responsibility.

Our franchisee model is very catchment centric wherein we offer a limited territory to them for operations. They manufacture and supply in that restricted area.

Small franchisees are hardworking and focused. Small concentrated market also reduces the transportation cost, which is a major expense for us as we have two-way transportation cost for glass bottles.

> **❝** Nearly every week we have proposal from VC's and equity investor's, IPO also is an option, but we think we are not yet ready internally. **❞**

We sell concentrates to them and they do production, bottling, marketing and sales. They also make money for themselves. We don't charge any royalty; we earn through selling concentrates to them.

We do QC audit periodically and keep our ears always open to all the customer complaints so that franchisees stay alert as well.

We have over 500 distributors and we cover over 95000 outlets across all the states in which we operate. 700 people are working for us and approximately 300 of them are in sales.

Since last 3 years, we have been rapidly growing, doubling our revenues each year.

We have a factory at Palsana, Surat, where we also produce flavored drinking water along with regular water. Approximately 4 % of our revenue come from exports.

Nearly every week we have proposal from VC's and equity investor's, IPO also is an option, but we think we are not yet ready internally.

Key growth factors:

Reasons behind the good growth in last 4 years are mainly, consistency in sales force, consistency in marketing efforts, strong focus on the quality and on R&D, regular market visits and services, strong efforts by local franchisees and above all, aggressive market expansion tactics.

The key success factor for us has been the constantly evolving product basket. We kept on adding new products with the time. You must be innovative to excel.

From glass bottles to pet to cans. From normal drinking water to flavored water, we kept on evolving with the time and have used the best possible technology and that is why we have survived in this market.

> ❝ *Our vision is to become a full-fledged Indian beverage company and want to spread across India. We are expanding in approximately 15 states in next couple of years.* ❞

Use of modern technology has helped us to be what we are today. We have pet blowing machines, new glass bottle machines, canning machines, In-house quality control lab, flavor concentrate production unit and many more. This differentiates us from many other local players of the domestic market.

Throughout the journey, our key strengths have been our loyal customers, teamwork, mutual efforts among the team members and the top management, consistent training and coaching to our people and above all, binding the team with organizational culture.

Future:

Our vision is to become a full-fledged Indian beverage company and want to spread across India.

We have plans ready to expand in approximately 15 states in next couple of years. We are also coming up with two new soft drink brands called "opener" and "Keychain"

Team's contribution

Our team has played the role of a catalyst in our success. They stood by us for years, struggled with us in good and bad times and many of them are still there, working tirelessly for the growth of this organization.

For any entrepreneur, it is imperative to be an excellent leader himself. Only then you should expect the excellence from your team.

As a leader I always guide my team to be 'responsible'. I encourage them to take responsibility of their family, of themselves, to be a responsible citizen for this country, for the company, for environment and above all, to be a responsible citizen of the society in which we live.

> **❝ I believe the new generation youth are much more advanced and intelligent than what we were. All we need to do is to develop a clear vision, coach them effectively and get out of their way. ❞**

I encourage them to work with a sense of 'ownership' 'loyalty' and 'discipline'. For company, country and for all the above mentioned stake holders

I myself, am a very disciplined person. I have studied in an army school so even today, my dressing, grooming and behavior are as per the requirements of the army

I believe the new generation youth are much more advanced and intelligent than what we were. All we need to do is to develop a clear vision, coach them effectively and get out of their way.

While hiring for sales, we never look for qualification; rather we look at skills and experience. This was taught to us by Mr. Jagdeep Kapoor, from Shamshika marketing.

Sports is another area where I encourage them to participate in. Sports is must; it develops the leadership qualities in you. It makes you a better manager, if you are part of team games.

I have always been in a position of leadership in my school and college days in whatever I did.

Social Life:

I was always passionate about leading or for being at the front. I was also involved in rotary for a while, worked for community institutions, taking care of the welfare of approximately 280 families. I have adopted kids from slums and educated them. I personally visit slums to identify such kids and ensure that they don't dropout.

Family Life:

We are a family of 7 sisters and 4 brothers. In immediate family, it's my wife, our two children and myself.

> **People think that consultants are expensive and their services add up unnecessary cost but they are wrong.**

My father used to keep telling me "be innovative, get the best technology, if you don't find good Indian machines, go for German machine but go out and do it."

Yet another piece of advice that he gave me was *'Din me rahke duniya ke sath chalo'* which means 'we should never forget the ethical principles and values taught by our religion, while doing business'.

My wife has adjusted a lot with me and unconditionally supported me throughout.

My son is innovative; he is aggressive in his skills and hungry for growth.

My Brother always said: "Don't make the mistakes that we did, take ready knowledge from different sources and grow faster"

Support of professional consultant:

Both my son and I have been regularly coached and mentored by Mr. Jagdeep Kapoor. He is a marketing consultant but has guided us in every way for all aspects of business since 2009. And that has been a major reason behind our rapid growth in the past few years.

A professional consultant helps us in strategic planning, marketing, branding, sales planning and management, HRM, suggests good names for products, develops catch-lines, helps us in media planning and above all mentors us in all aspects. They facilitate growth.

People think that consultants are expensive and their services add up unnecessary cost but they are wrong.

Because of their false belief, they don't go for professional help. Thus, people like us who take professional help, get the benefit of the inaction of these average thinkers.

> **I believe that without education, you can't stand out in this world.**

If you have a consultant and 'if' you follow their advice, they are not expensive, rather they add lot of value. At times their fees comes out from the innovative ideas they suggest. We don't pay them from our pockets.

We spend approximately 4% to 5% of our sales amount on marketing.

My thoughts on education:

Education was critical to my success and same is true for everyone. I believe that without education, you can't stand out in this world.

I got admission in London and everything was set. But suddenly I realized that I have spent lot of time in hostel staying away from family. Thus, I turned down that opportunity and later, I joined KC College and was studying with Mr. Anil Ambani in same class.

There too, I quit my studies because science had nothing to do with my business. But my mother insisted that I get educated and under her persistence I studied here at Surat.

People from whom I draw my inspiration are:

Firstly, my father. I learnt a lot from him. I've learnt the values like hard work and wisdom from him.

Next is my friend Gurindar Singh Bhatija, a sardarji from Pune. He once told me "Abbas modernize, don't stretch, go for advance technologies". He changed my perspective and I was able to take major decisions in my life for the business.

My advice to other entrepreneurs is:

- Use best of the available technology
- Be an excellent leader yourself and live a disciplined life
- Develop good team, coach them and trust them with all the execution responsibilities.
- Focus very hard on market dynamics and marketing and
- Finally, be very ethical in your business and also in your personal life.

SAILING ON THE DIGITAL WAVES

Mr. Sanjeev Bhatia
Co-Founder

Firm Name:
Bhatia's Mobile

Estd:1996

Products or Services

Mobile and other digital gadget retailing and Partner of 'HSL' Brand of Mobile phones

In the digital gadgets retailing industry of the western part of India, Bhatia Mobiles is a widely renowned name. But it was Mr. Sanjeev Bhatia's powerful vision and determination that led him to this stature, despite all odds. He transformed a simple STD PCO venture into a brand that is the leading retailer of digital gadgets. They have recently launched their own brand of cell phones 'HSL' and are all set to revolutionize the domestic cell phone market.

Bhatia Mobiles

"There were many competitors, they were pioneers and much stronger than us. They entered into this business earlier than us but could not grow big. The key difference between them and us were two;

1. *Marketing*
2. *They did not change with the time, they were not flexible and responsive to the emerging market opportunities."*

………. Sanjeev Bhatia

"India sells 1 crore cell phones every month", says Mr. Sanjeev Bhatia, the man who along with his brother created a retail brand of digital products retailing, 'Bhatia Mobiles' which has 85 running stores today. They also have their own brand of cell phones 'HSL'.

Reflecting on past Mr. Sanjeev narrated about how this journey started.

We had textile business in family but my father met with an accident and was under treatment for 3 years. During that period the textile business collapsed and we were in heavy debts. We had to sell all our assets to repay the debts.

Since my father was handicapped, he got the license for STD PCO. In 1990, we started with STD PCO, Xerox, gift items and juice center etc. all in one shop at ring road, Surat.

> *Every adversity has an opportunity.*

With time and experience we realized that the gift articles business had greater scope thus we focused more on that category and gradually closed all the other services.

After 1995 with the launch of cell phone services in India, emerged a new opportunity for us, and that was about sales and service of cell phones, sales of accessories, pre-paid and postpaid connections and pre-paid recharge. Accessories amongst all the above, was much more lucrative and had repeat sales on each cell phone purchase. It had great potential so we decided to focus more on this category.

We started purchasing the accessories from the direct importers and also went abroad personally for purchase. But once due to lack of knowledge about customs and other procedures, our goods worth Rs.20 lakhs were held.

One of the local newspaper wrote a full page on this issue to harass us. But instead, we got a huge benefit out of it. It was like a free publicity. Because of this article whole Surat came to know that we are genuine importers of original accessories and thus our business started prospering.

Every adversity has an opportunity.

Change with the time:

We kept on changing with the time. Since 2002 the sales of mobile phone started shooting and thus we closed all our services and converted to full fledge mobile phone and digital products retailing.

In those days, we also used to buy second-hand phones and re-sell it. But some people in market spread the rumor that Bhatia renews old phones and sells it at the cost of new. As soon as we came to know about it, we immediately decided and stopped dealing in second-hand phones. Because brand image takes years to develop, but few minutes to collapse.

> *Customer satisfaction, service, quality and marketing are the key to success.*

Even in repairing service business, when we found that, we are unable to deliver it on time and deliver satisfactory performance through our service and repairing, in spite of healthy profits we closed down the repairing service and now we solely focus on selling cell phones and accessories.

As time was moving ahead, we sensed the opportunity to scale in other parts of the city and South Gujarat region. Hence, we started opening more stores to create a chain of store under the brand name of 'Bhatia mobiles'.

We have both; company owned retail stores as well as franchisees. Currently around 85 stores are running successfully.

Focus on Marketing:

Customer satisfaction, service, quality and marketing are the key to success.

Initially I took one full year to decide whether to spend on marketing or not, but once I made up my mind, I have never looked back. Now we are consistent in our marketing efforts and actively' use all the possible online and offline media to promote our store brand. We are a very aggressive marketer now.

This we have learnt from my father; he was a very good marketer. Even when we had a juice center, he actively used to do scooter branding and almost one in every four-scooter had our advertisement on it. Thus, we were very famous in market.

We encashed this awareness of our old business into our mobile phone retailing business.

Franchising:

We launched our franchisee module in 2007, and appointed initial 5 franchisees. They earned fair returns and thus we started getting more

> **❝** *I give major credit of my success to marketing, risk taking, scaling at right time and flexibility to change with the time.* **❞**

inquiries. Soon we had more than 50 franchisees + 35 company owned outlets in the entire South Gujarat region

Initially mobile phone retail business could be done with Rs.10 lakh capital because the phone price range was between 1000 to max 20000. But today the good selling smart phone price range starts from 20k and goes up to 65k and thus this business has become capital intensive and it can't be done with lesser capital.

The other aspect of this business is that, you can't run it without stock. Thus, many of the initial franchisees that started with lesser capital and could not invest more were converted to company owned outlets. As per current status, we have 25 franchisees and remaining 60 are the company-managed stores.

Fighting Competition:

There were many competitors, they were pioneers and much stronger than us. They entered this business earlier than us but could not grow big. The key difference between them and us were two;

1. Marketing
2. They did not change with the time. They were not flexible and responsive to the emerging market opportunities.

They focused only on profitability, which was shrinking due to price war. They did not focus on increasing their customer base. Thus, in spite of being older than us, they remained small and mostly single store operation business.

Many of them thought, repairing business is more profitable then selling new phones, and they still are behind repairing. But even from that lot, many of them don't market and are not focusing on increasing their customer base, neither they are operating from multiple locations.

> **❝** Out of 10 marketing ideas that we applied, 7 failed, but the remaining 3 produced excellent results and gave us good returns. **❞**

There are few who diverted to sales of Chinese phones, just because it had better margins. They did not want to sell Samsung or iPhone because it had less profitability.

Key Success Factor:

I give major credit of my success to marketing, risk taking, scaling at right time and flexibility to change with the time.

I always focused on marketing and increasing our customer base. Because of which, even in low margin era, our performance has been fair.

Even in marketing, we did not know anything, but we learnt through lot of experimentation. Out of 10 marketing ideas that we applied, 7 failed, but the remaining 3 produced excellent results and gave us good returns.

Our catch-line "Ab Mobile Bikega Toh Bhatia Se Hi Bikega" is very popular. We are using it in every commercial and since many years. This communicates our attitude to the market. It communicates our passion and desire to sell to each customer and indirectly that is our sole mission too.

Early struggle days:

Initially my mom, dad & younger brother all were involved in this business along with me. But now my younger brother and I are managing it. My dad still takes care of marketing and esp. wall branding in entire South Gujarat.

I started working from the age of 13 while I was in 7th standard. I used to go to school in the morning and manage the store post lunch. I was also travelling to Mumbai and Delhi for gift article purchase along with my younger brother who was of 11 years at that time.

The relatives and other people in surrounding used to reprimand my father for sending such small kids of 13 and 11 years for purchase. To which,

> **The offline retailing is not completely gone, we believe it will stay for many decades to come and thus, we wish to open more stores in areas where the online buyers are less**

my father used to smile and reply, "I am not sending two kids of age 13 and 11, rather I am actually sending 1 person of age 24 [13 + 11= 24 years]."

I also went to Singapore and Hong Kong for purchasing at the age of 22 while I was in college. But despite of my involvement in business and having huge responsibility on my shoulder, I still managed to complete my SSC and HSC and also enrolled for CA studies but dropped after couple of years. My younger brother however managed to complete his graduation. He did B.Com.

At present, I take care of business expansion, marketing, planning and sales. My brother takes care of HR and operations. We also have in house LED board making company which produces all our marketing and branding material

Launch of HSL:

Around 2012, I realized that the sales of Indian brands were growing. esp. Micromax, Intex, Lava and Karbon etc. In Bhatia's stores we were selling approx. 6000 to 7000 such phones a year. Based on this observation, we decided to launch our own brand of phones under the brand 'HSL'. It was launched two years back and had sales of 20000 units and 33 crore revenue last financial year.

We have high hopes for this brand, as there is a good market for low cost smart phones in India, esp. in rural areas. I had ready market through our own retail chain and now we are developing a sales and distribution channel to further scale the sales of this brand.

We partly own 'HSL' as we have another partner as joint owner.

Current status:

Today we are generating revenues of Rs. 33 crores from HSL while Bhatia mobiles is doing annual Rs. 170 crore business, selling approx. 20k phones every month.

> **Mujhe sale karna nahi aata hai, mujhe sale karvana aata hai**

Approx. 30% to 35% of quality customers from entire market, are buying from us.

Online Opportunity:

With growing popularity of online retailing, traditional retailers are afraid and look at it as a threat. Online is a threat as well as an opportunity for us. They kill our retailing business of other brands but they also sell our HSL products in large numbers, which will exponentially grow with the time.

The offline retailing is not completely gone, we believe it will stay for many decades to come and thus, we wish to open more stores in areas where the online buyers are less, and there are many such pockets.

We are launching our mobile application and starting our own online sales portal with the promise to deliver products within 6 hours. Other online retailers deliver within 3 to 4 working days.

Market domination and leadership is our mission. Our advertisements are targeted to the common man and are purposefully designed to be little funny but catchy.

"Mujhe sale karna nahi aata hai, mujhe sale karvana aata hai" [I don't know how to sell, but I definitely know how to get effective sales from others]

Team does everything:

Our major success factor has been building and managing good quality team.

Flexibility to change with the time, sharp focus on customer satisfaction, delegating to the team and coaching them effectively & above all giving them good earning opportunities through incentives are other progressive routes. All this has resulted in our growth.

At the end of the day, we just give targets, guidance and policy framework but the entire execution and operation is managed by and

> **But I would still say that mistakes are a major source of learning and we must make more mistakes to learn more from it**

executed by the team. Team does everything and thus, we give lot of appreciation and credit to them and take great care of them.

Approx. 600 people work for us. Our core team is made up of hundred people; we take care of their insurance and the education of their children.

Learning from mistakes:

Every entrepreneur makes mistakes before succeeding. We too have made many. Fortunately, there aren't too many threatening mistakes. But yes, we have done lot of trial and error in marketing, lot of our campaigns have failed, but we have learnt a lot from each of those failures.

The other mistake was the wrong selection of few of the store locations. To correct those mistakes, we had to spend lot of money in marketing for developing decent sales. After that, we have been very careful about selecting the locations.

One big mistake in life was the launching of the online portal, for which we did marketing worth 35 lakh rupees on offline medias but could not even sell products worth 3.5 lakh. It was a big loss, but also a big learning. I realized that to sell online, you must promote your products online.

But I would still say that mistakes are a major source of learning and we must make more mistakes to learn more from it. Never try to play safe or avoid mistakes.

The biggest failure in life is that you have never failed.

Use of Technology:

To ensure profitable operations, one must be very efficient and vigilant & for that we have developed our own customized software to manage the business. We had invested Rs.17 lakh for the development of this software.

> **❝ Business aapko naam aur pehchan deta hai, satisfaction deta hai, aur isse bahot learning milti hai ❞**

Technology is the key to success. It is not possible to manage a business without technology.

Today I get real time data, anytime. This helps me in pricing control, stock transfer, stock management etc... It helps me to know the store and product performance and overall business management. It also helps in quick decision making for the business.

We also have used technology to the fullest for marketing purpose.

Future:

We never did business for high profits and bigger sales. We have a very small family and have enough to sustain it. Our target is market domination and leadership.

Definitely the future plan is that; every important lane of the city and surrounding areas should have a Bhatia store.

For HSL we are planning to cover entire India through sales and distribution channel and we also are getting aggressive with the online sales of it. We have recently signed Priety Zinta as our brand ambassador

Why business?

I do business to keep myself busy, it is my passion. I can't stay without my business.

"Business aapko naam aur pehchan deta hai, satisfaction deta hai, aur isse bahot learning milti hai"

[Business gives you name and fame, it also gives you satisfaction and lot of learning's]

I have always learnt a lot through my business. i.e. HSL taught me that if you sell a phone, you will also have to give service and repair back up. So we have done a tie up with a mobile phone repair company, which is

> **❝** *In tough times, no one will support you so don't expect help from others. Believe in yourself and learn to come out of the tough situation on your own.* **❞**

servicing our phones at 440 locations in India. Business teaches me new things every day.

Investment minded people, who look for investment in properties or stocks of other companies instead of investing those funds into their own business, are very small thinkers and they remain small. They will never grow beyond a particular point.

Role of family in our success:

Family definitely plays a very important role in entrepreneur's success. so is with me.

My father and mother were the greatest support right from day one. Later, we both brothers have been great support to each other. We have worked hand in hand from childhood.

200 days in a year I eat out and I am not with the family and in my absence it is my wife who manages the family. She manages the family and all other social responsibilities and thus I am able to concentrate on the growth of my company. Without the support of my wife, my business would not thrive, nor would I be able to enjoy my life.

Social Contribution:

We have contributed for several social causes as per our capacity. We take care of education of a few needy kids and also donated for the construction of hospitals.

Some personal thoughts

Key learning of my life that I acquired is; in tough times, no one will support you so don't expect help from others. Instead, believe in yourself and take charge of your life. Learn to come out of the tough situation on your own.

> **❝** You can't always rely only on your CA and advisor for everything. You must have the basic idea of all the relevant issues related to your business **❞**

My role models are my father and Mr. Govind from SYSKA LED.

My father, in spite of being handicapped, used to work on juice center along with my mom till 2 am and then at 4 am they used to go to fruit market for the purchases. He never stopped working. This is a very important learning and has been an inspiration for me. They taught me that no matter what, never stop working. Hard work is essential for our growth.

I met Mr. Govind for the first time in 2008. He is one of the leading dealers of Samsung mobile phones in India. He created a strong sales channel for Samsung in India and now has launched his own brand 'SYSKA LED'

Basic education and awareness is must. You can't always rely only on your CA and advisor for everything. You must have the basic idea of all the relevant issues related to your business so that you can manage the business well and independently.

I don't believe in learning futile subjects. One should focus on and learn only the most relevant subjects and develop specialization accordingly.

Meeting people and learning from them is also education. And this is the best path for any entrepreneur.

My advice to other entrepreneurs is:

- 'Never give up'. Be consistent and persistent. Your progress at times; is determined by the others giving up. They give up and you get an opportunity. Likewise, if you give up, you give opportunity to others to grow. Never lose hope and keep trying.

PASSION FOR CUSTOMER SATISFACTION

Mr. Sandeep Dawer

Founder

Firm Name:

Sugar 'N' Spice

Estd: 1998

Products or Services

Restaurants and Food Services

A self-made man, Mr. Sandeep Dawer created a food chain, whose fame and business has spread to every nook and corner of Gujarat and other parts of the country. Instead of following his father's footsteps as a doctor, he chose to start his own multi-cuisine food chain that has become the favorite eating out destination in several parts of India.

Sugar 'N' Spice

"More than the profits, the happiness of the customers matters to us."

.... Sandeep Dawer

The man filled with passion and full of consumer insights, Mr. Sandeep Dawer is the first generation entrepreneur who developed several formats and brands and is all set to dominate the restaurant industry with rapid expansion.

In the personal chat, he candidly mentioned his interesting story on creating an enterprise and how he defied the odds and emerged as the proud owner of one of the most popular food service companies of Gujarat.

I did MBA from Delhi and in 1998 came to Surat. Dad was an eye surgeon at Agra and I had option of joining his profession. I had only two options; either to do a job or start my own business. I chose the latter.

Those days Agra had a problem of water, electricity & law and order. For me it was not a good option to do business at Agra so I came to Surat. Here we had a property in dawer chambers at ring road, Surat. I decided to do something in this property and restaurant was the first thought.

The relatives at Surat thought that it was a bad decision. They said, *"Baap ka 20 se 25 lakh duboyega aur vapas chala jayega"* (he will incur losses worth 20-25 lakhs, reduce assets of his father and then go back).

> **❝** *If you are a resident of Surat and have not visited 'Sugar 'N' Spice' then it is as if you have committed a crime.* **❞**

Today the same relatives proudly say *'Hamara baccha hai'* [he is our kid]. The attitude and approach of people changes with time and success.

Business Establishment and Expansion:

'Sugar 'N' Spice' was our first venture and it has been a huge success, even till date no other restaurant is as popular as Sugar 'N' Spice in entire South Gujarat region. If you are a resident of Surat and have not visited 'Sugar 'N' Spice' then it is as if you have committed a crime. It's been 16 years and till date we have no competition in this format.

It is the only place where you get kababs, kathi rolls, veg-non-veg Punjabi, Indian, Chinese, tandoori kababs, grills, biryani, Rogan gost and other Mughlai dishes. You also get pizzas, burgers, sandwiches, garlic bread, French fries, deserts etc. all under one roof.

Elsewhere you don't get non-veg Chinese, Chicken sandwiches, pizzas burgers etc. Either you go to Golden Dragon (which is another reputed Chinese restaurant of Surat for non-veg Chinese) or go to roadside thela for such stuff but you have no other restaurant serving these.

Topographically we are at the wrong location, on a commercial street. Yet, we are doing a wonderful business.

In the year 2000 we created 'Deewane Khas', a pure veg restaurant with typical Punjabi taste. This too was a huge success.

Through both our restaurants, we brought typical Delhi taste to Surat.

Just by preparing onion tomato gravy and adding paneer will not make it a paneer butter masala, what changes the taste is the use of right masalas, The other ingredients like onion, tomato capsicum would be same in all the dishes.

At Deewane Khas, first 2 months we got no response, but after that, next 9 months we had people queuing up every day. Now, on any day it is a minimum of 45 minutes waiting before one can get a seat. People have

> ❝ *There are very few successful players in Gujarat. Apart from 'Sugar 'N' Spice', only Havmor, Honest and Sankalp are popular chains and have decent product range.* ❞

stopped coming on weekends so that at least they don't have to wait for more than an hour.

Little after that, we went on to put up a pastry shop at the Parle point area of Surat. It was a backward integration for us, as we required lot of breads in our restaurants and the supply was uneven. Taste consistency was also a challenge. Hence we decided to put up our own production and on a parallel scale, started selling pastries in our restaurants and also opened a retail outlet.

We have around 9 pastry shops running today. We always try to be different than others and offer innovative or different products to the market.

In those days' people knew only chocolate pastries and some regular flavors. The cassata pastry and many other varieties are our gift to the city. Once we started, rest of the bakers copied us and the citizens of the city started benefiting from this process.

Then we launched 'Utsav' banquet hall but it did not work well so we converted it into a fine dining restaurant 'Taste of India' in 2004. It offers unlimited buffet for both veg and non-veg food lovers. The 'Taste of India' too is very popular in the city and is a very successful format for us.

There are very few successful players in Gujarat. Apart from 'Sugar 'N' Spice', only Havmor, Honest and Sankalp are popular chains and have decent product range.

We were so famous that Bejan Daruwala the famous astrologer drove down to Surat to have food at our place. Even the film stars travelling to Surat for different programs and events used to stay at Taj Gateway but they used to order food from our restaurant.

Ismail Darbar, Pankaj Dheer were regular with Sugar 'N' Spice whenever they travelled to Surat. And Sudha Shiv Puri, Smriti Irani have visited Deewane Khas.

> **"** *Because of our burger, sales of Mcdonalds dropped by 40% and they sent their team to Surat to study the reasons.* **"**

Burger Mania:

In 2007 we started express counters at different locations of Surat city. We launched Burger at only rupees 10/-. It was so popular that we had to keep two security guards at each counter along with steel grills so that the public does not rush onto our team members. There was long queue at all four outlets that were serving Rs. 10 burger. It rocked the city and awareness about the brand that it generated was the major gain.

The rationale behind this was that if a Vada pav can be sold at Rs.5/-, Why can't we try selling a burger at Rs. 10/-?

Because of our burger, sales of Mcdonalds dropped by 40% and they sent their team to Surat to study the reasons. One of the friend from marketing industry called and said; 'What have you done, you have forced people from Mcdonalds to spend huge money on local marketing'.

Sharp focus on customer satisfaction is the key:

People want 'naya' and 'achha' (hygiene & variety).

The all-important question for restaurant business is, what can you do to give people change and happiness?

People always look for a change. Khana toh har kisike ghar me bhi banta hai, phir bhi they are willing to spend twice or thrice amount just for a change and enjoyment

If you focus on customer needs, they will come back and give you repeat business and that will lead you to success. Money is not the motto – motto always is to satisfy need of people and send them back with happiness.

> ❝ We have added some 24 locations in last 3 years out of which 11 were in last year. ❞

Our offerings to the customers are very simple; Reasonable price, excellent quality, new varieties and clean infrastructure.

Current status:

We have 7 diff. restaurant formats & we stand top in terms of systems and management.

Our current formats are 'Sugar 'N' Spice', 'Deewane Khas', 'Taste of India' 'Sub Stations' 'Pizza format' 'Swad Sangam' 'Highway Format'. We have 36 outlets running across all formats

We serve the largest cuisine varieties in India. No one serves the number of cuisines we offer.

We also have our catering services – but do some selective events. We are not so keen on it.

Till 2012 we had some 12 locations, now we have 36. We have added some 24 locations in last 3 years out of which 11 were in last year.

Our highway format is on the lines of Haldiram, where you get all cuisines, multiple varieties for each age group and segment, all under one roof.

There was a need gap, because on highways there were only dhabas and no organized players. This is one of the best formats and is super successful. We are planning a meaningful expansion with this format.

We saw only 3 organized players on highway, McDonalds, Dominos and Café Coffee Day. Now we have started.

The current locations are smartly selected, as they are right in the middle of the Surat-Mumbai highway, between Surat-Ahmedabad, between Ahmedabad-Rajkot. And the chances for travelers to halt and relax in between are better.

The property between Ahmedabad and Rajkot is newly developed and it is one of the most beautiful hotel properties in India. Not just in western India

> **We want them to be happy while dinning and be happy when they move out. Profit is important but not more than the happiness of a customer.**

Even the one, which is between Surat and Baroda. It is at par with MNC's

Here we use the bone china crockery, tabletop, wooden chairs and the services are one of the best in India. We give menu of casual dining and give you experience of semi fine dinning.

The toilets should be always maintained as new. The idea is to give good atmosphere, good ambience, good food and an enjoyable experience.

We want them to be happy while dinning and be happy when they move out. Profit is important but not more than the happiness of a customer.

Shortly we are opening at Baroda, Pune, and Hyderabad. Accommodating Café Coffee Day and McDonalds in our properties. We are opening our restaurants very soon in following territories and cities. Gujarat, Union Territory - Selvasa, Maharashtra, Rajasthan Delhi-Jaipur highway, Varanasi.

We are also in talks with couple of overseas investors and would launch some of our formats at Australia & Dubai.

Key Challenges:

We have decided not to increase express counters anymore, because the employee attrition and Quality Control are the big issues. As we train people, they leave. And if your people keep on changing, maintaining consistent quality is a big challenge. Dominos, Pizza Hut, CCD too are closing down their express counters, for the same reasons.

Small formats in India are not working because in India, labor laws are not supportive. In some of the countries, the person has to submit the documents and also have to avail the clearance certificate before opting for the other job. Here we don't have such practice or policies.

On 1st of the month, the person will take the salary and suddenly on 2nd he will not appear, if we inquire, he will say he has joined another job.

> **" We invite expert chefs, also from 5 star hotels and train our people through them. We train our people a lot. "**

Even the cooks leave suddenly and at times you have to cook food yourself as an owner or close certain cuisine abruptly.

Ours is not the business where you can manufacture in extra shift and settle the production loss. Here everything is live, spot cooking, spot serving, spot experience and if right person is not there at the right place, you are gone.

Team management is the most painful area. Every new restaurant that starts, they try to snatch our people. But we have excellent relations with all our people. We ask our people to bring their chacha, mama, brothers, cousins and other relatives, and they happily bring them.

Soon we are opening two outlets and we need 150 people. but we already have a long waiting list of people who want to work with us.

I don't pay high, in fact, I pay 10% lesser than the market but with us there is consistency of work, we give them respect, we treat them with equality, if they go to their villages and return even after 3 months, we give them work. So, they have job security.

We invite expert chefs, also from 5 star hotels and train our people through them. We train our people a lot.

We were the first to start pizzas with mozzarella cheese, barbeque burger and many other products, years ahead of Dominos, Pizza Hut and McDonalds

At present 1600 people are working for us and will be 2000 very soon.

85% properties are making profits and 15% are struggling due to heavy rentals. Rentals are the major expense, so now we have decided that we will not do any restaurant on rental property. In rentals, only the property owner earns, on our efforts.

Constant R&D is our key success factor:

What made us successful till date is our R&D that we do for constant search and development of new cuisines and varieties.

> *If someone is doing good, we will study their cuisine, do R&D and develop our dish with our quality standards.*

Customers today are highly experimental and they search for new varieties all the time. They need new items in each of their outings.

"Shahrukh 7 din me buddha nahi ho jata par phir bhi 7th day ke baad uski movie ka craze khatam hota hai, kyuki koi aur new movie aa jati hai" [Shahrukh doesn't grow old within a week yet his movie generates weak business from 2nd week, because some other new movie is released and the crowd chases the new]

At one point of time chat-panipuri, aaloo tikki and chillas were the major attraction at marriages now most of the marriages has live pasta counters. With times people need new things.

To keep ourselves updated with market trends, we learn from self, from customers, we learn from other players in our industry.

If someone is doing good, we will study their cuisine, do R&D and develop our dish with our quality standards. We are serving all the possible latest varieties in our restaurants. We offer lazaniya, tacos, pasta, chilladas, nachos etc.

I study the multinationals and their strategies. They launch 4 to 6 new products each year and keep 1 or 2 most successful and kill the rest. We also follow some of the best practices of Dominos, Pizza Hut, McDonalds.

McDonalds launches one new product in summer and one compulsorily in the diwali vacations.

The timing of R&D has to be right. Before time or after others will both result in loss.

People advice me that start high-end non-veg restaurant, but I know it will not work. If I launch lobsters with 1200 rs. Or dosa in a silver plate at 200 rs, it will not work. Never forget the basics and fundamentals of market. Look at what current market is ready for and launch only those things.

> **" I am not afraid of MNC's; I can handle them. "**

Even in multiplexes, if you have six screens, all are not luxurious, only one is. At best, in a particular screen only one row is luxurious with recliner seats not all rows.

Why jaguar does not have showroom in Surat? Because the number of units to be sold is less, so it is catered from Mumbai showroom.

Focus is always on quality. No mixing of any other impure material. Our sweets are prepared in pure desi ghee. We have a very high checking process for taste and quality. We take great care at the time of purchase and check all the materials received. We are very strict in vendor selection. If the purchase of material is good, the quality will definitely be good.

I was not from this industry, yet I managed it, because business is all about passion. I myself have become a good cook doing lot of R&D.

Every outlet that you see is my own interior designed I am that much involved into this business and am too passionate about.

Fighting Competition:

I am not afraid of MNC's; I can handle them. There are many who serve soya bean instead of chicken in the sandwich.

Softy is frozen desert it does not fall into ice cream category. It is nothing but a mixture of milk powder with oil & some essence. We know how to tackle them.

Our major concern is lari galla – road side thela. They are low price, poor hygiene, poor quality, they don't have operational expenditure as we have and yet we are most of the time compared with their cost.

They don't have manpower, infrastructure, liabilities, taxes, quality standards, rental etc. and municipal corporations too are not that much of keen on controlling them.

Locations are the key: we opened a restaurant at a location, which is densely populated at Varachha [Surat] area with population of 10 lakhs or

> *Making quick money is not my drive. Sugar 'N' Spice is my baby and I don't want to sell my baby. Because now, it is not about only me, it's about my entire team.*

more. We thought it would produce good business, but it turned out to be a bad decision and we are struggling over there. In spite of that property being one of the finest properties of Surat.

Future

We have no set targets – we are focused on how many outlets we can open successfully and be profitable.

We often get offers from PE investors. They ask us to take money, cover pan India and in few years they would like to encash and move out.

This is not how I want to work. I don't want to work for their money and profits, I want it my way. Once I take their money, I would be working for their returns and not for my passion. So I deny such offers.

Making quick money is not my drive. Sugar 'N' Spice is my baby and I don't want to sell my baby. Because now, it is not about only me, it's about my entire team.

Our Contribution to Society and Nation:

I think I am contributing a lot through my business: I am creating jobs, I am paying taxes, I am developing a good Indian brand, we are training so many people through our business and above all we are giving quality food at affordable rates to the customers.

We want to give much better experience, food and happiness to all our customers who have made us what we are today.

"*Business se is desh ka vikas hota hai*" (A country develops through successful business ventures.)

On the social sector, we ran a campaign on world environment day 'Aao ek paudha lagaye' some 2000 saplings were planted. We spent around 4 lakhs rupees behind it.

> **Kids will do what they like? Let them follow their passion. This business is my passion, so they also have the right to follow their passion.**

We are also developing one of the best fountains of India at 'Y' junction near VR Mall, Surat. We are developing it with SMC. This will be the feather in the crown of this city. It would be the asset for this city. This city has given me so much, I must give back to it.

Family Support:

My Family has been a great support to me. They never intrude or interfere. No unwanted suggestions, full support.

My travelling is more, late night working is common, in spite of this, they never stopped me from expanding the business.

As far as my kids are concerned and whether they will join this business or not? Kids will do what they like? Let them follow their passion. This business is my passion, so they also have the right to follow their passion.

Atmosphere in the family has to be great and such that, it promote learning. Let your children go out, explore, expose themselves to the world and learn a lot. Don't put them into shells. Encourage your children to go for best possible education. Education gives you necessary exposure.

My Advice to other entrepreneurs would be:

- Go ahead in a rightful manner, never indulge into unethical practices.
- Never be afraid of losses – it's part of life. Not all reliance business is successful and Sachin also don't score a century in every match.
- Take calculated risk and keep debt in manageable range. Don't over burden yourself with debt. Greater the debt, greater the risk.
- Whatever you do? Do it wholeheartedly. Or else don't at all do it. Some people do business but for trying half-heartedly and thus it fails. If you do? Do with complete faith or else don't do. Do it with full might.

TOWARDS A GREENER AND CLEANER TOMORROW

Mr. Girish Luthra

Chairman & CEO

Firm Name:

Luthra Group

Estd: 1980

Products & Services

Dyeing Printing Mills & Environment Solutions

For Mr. Girish Luthra, the challenge was to overcome the sharp drop in revenues in their business and transform their line of production into a more sustainable pattern. On the personal front, he had foregone his engineering degree to hold reins to the business but he consistently tried to acquire knowledge in the entire span of his career. Today, he not only is invited to the reputed institutions including IIM's for speeches but also is at the apex of a highly successful and popular textile and environment solution companies, 'LUTHRA' & 'GEPIL'

Luthra Group

"Normally the success of an enterprise is measured through its balance sheet, but our success is measured through green balance sheet, which reflects how much waste have we managed & helped for environment protection."

.... Girish Luthra

Mr. Girish Luthra is a 2nd generation entrepreneur. An inventor, an avid learner and a very strong willed person. He leads two organizations; Luthra and GEPIL. He is frequently invited to speak at various management institutes including IIM Ahmedabad and Kolkata. He is an active member of CII and has also been the committee member with planning commission of India. Let's read his story in his own words.

My father started the business. He came to Surat and worked for some local company. Later, in 1963 he started his own weaving unit. In 80's we decided to go for processing, thus my father asked me to go for related education. In 1999 we launched GEPIL, an environment solution company.

Initial Years of My Life:

I joined industry in 1981 after diploma in textile chemicals. Actually I wanted a degree in engineering but had to let go my degree due to my

> **❝ Textile industry of Surat is operating with very narrow mind and traditional thoughts. We are still very unorganized, we are still in nothing but a large village culture ❞**

presence required in my father's business. But I also committed myself that, someday my knowledge and ability would be greater than anyone else in my field and one day, I will deliver the lectures to the engineering students.

While studying, I was not allowed to go by bike or a scooter for safety reasons and my father had a small business, so I had to travel by luna because it was slow and safe, no chance of accident. Later, I got second-hand jeep, while many of my friends travelled by better cars and flashy bikes. Even whose father could not afford? But I am happy to be grown that way, seen and experienced the harsh weather and faced all the tough challenges, which made me what I am today. That experience has kind of prepared me for the harsh realities of life.

When I entered the business, I observed that everything is unorganized and there was no sign of professionalism. There were high chances of getting cheated at every step, if you lack knowledge.

When I wanted to set up a lab and started searching for advice and help, I could not get the proper compiled information on that subject; there were no reply to any of my queries from anywhere. I understood the gap and decided to take charge and started documenting it on my own.

My father always used to guide me that no work is small, you must learn to do everything.

Textile industry of Surat is operating with very narrow mind and traditional thoughts. We are still very unorganized, we are still in nothing but a large village culture and hence we don't have the necessary professionalism. We don't have any system orientation.

There was also, the herd, mentality and I'll share an interesting example of this.

When our production scaled, we required washing machines, we went out and asked existing entrepreneurs for advice. We asked them, why they

> **The first and major challenge with 2nd or 3rd generation of entrepreneurs is that father or senior team members don't listen to you and take you very casually.**

bought? And how they were using? But they had no idea about proper use of it, they said others bought so we bought, or we were offered these machines along with other purchases.

Then I went to MANTRA [Man Made Textile Research Association] and along with them we went out to survey in other cities about the use of this technology. After lot of effective learning and with the support of key members from MANTRA, I designed a machine concept' which was more suitable to our local needs and was simple to use. We shared our concept and asked some of the manufacturers to develop the machine for us, based on our own concept.

That technology worked very well and the industry accepted it wholeheartedly. This episode gave me lot of confidence about my own abilities at a very young age.

My 2nd biggest challenge was internal. When I joined the family business, there were lot of senior and experienced people who did not readily accept my ideas and me. They said, *"kaal no chhokro mane bhanavse?"* [This toddler will teach us?].

The first and major challenge with 2nd or 3rd generation of entrepreneurs is that father or senior team members don't listen to you and take you very casually. Patience was the only option.

Meanwhile, I did lot of short term courses on management and learnt lot of concept like Management By Objectives etc. on the other hand I was reading about lot of technical developments that were happening within textile industry and the world at large.

I shared these learnings and ideas with the team but initially people rejected these ideas saying that this will not work in our industry. But at the later stage when they faced problems, they came to me for the solutions and that is how I got accepted by them as a good leader.

The harsh reality is that today's children are the product of protected environment and they are not shown the reality.

> *When I train somebody, I get trained myself.*

These days the business and the income have grown, but number of children in family has dropped to 1 to 2 kids and thus, they are given all the comfort by parents and are pampered and protected a lot. I tell them to be ready to get kicked off, keep your butts ready.

My Development Years:

MANTRA was working on color matching system and it was not getting established. This was an opportunity for me, since, I had taken some training on color matching. I worked with them post 6pm (after factory hours) and established it in 3 months. It was a wonderful learning experience for me as well.

After this I started documenting about lab operations and how to conduct certain tests in a very simple language. The industry people don't like to read, so I had to be very simple and the document had to be shortest. I wrote lot of articles on this and finally, all the articles got compiled and it got published as a book.

In 1993, the book got published "handbook for textile processor's" by MANTRA. Mr. Bapu Deshpandey, from Colourtex was the co-author. He checked all the content, did correction and added some content to it through his experience.

By that time my lab too got bigger and I had five technicians working in it. My age at that time was exactly 30 years.

That learning curve of continuously reading, writing and training had helped me a lot and kept me engaged with latest trends and technological developments. When I train somebody, I get trained myself.

Your friend circle has to be like minded. A technician can be very comfortable with other technical minds. And that is how I developed friendship with lot of technically sound people and all this helped me a lot in later years.

> **❝** It is my experience that even if you go out to serve others, in the process, you personally get lot of learning's and opportunity. **❞**

Attraction towards Environment Solutions:

While 80's was all about basic learning and experimentations, 90's was all about energy and environment.

Once established in the business and streamlined the operations, I decided to go for environmental studies. Minimizing the waste at the source in textiles, to save environmental damage and for cost reduction. That was the mission.

Due to our environmental study, Myself, Mr. Chitranjan Desai and one more person along with us, were invited to demonstrate our project for waste reduction in textile at USA in United Nations Project Desire Conference. The invitation came for only Mr. Chitranjan Desai, but he insisted, that it is the work of three people and we will go, only if we all three are invited. After a week we all three got an invitation to visit that conference.

Actually we three together had created waste minimization group. Our idea behind this group was to experiment on our own for 'waste reduction in textile' and then publish the material for industry to practice and follow. We had worked on this for one year and later we presented a paper in joint Indo-US conference at New Delhi and thus were invited for UN conference. Chitranjan Desai presented a paper.

That conference was a great learning and experience. We learnt a lot about waste management in textiles. After that conference, we became UN experts on Textile and Environment and we went on to serve the Industry.

It is my experience that even if you go out to serve others, in the process, you personally get lot of learnings and opportunity.

While I was involved into all this, along with managing my business, other players of Industry thought that all this was a waste of time. Baniya mindset ,forces people to think that anything that is not profitable, would be wastage of time.

> **❝ At that point of my life I realized that we should never chase money, chase knowledge and money will follow you. ❞**

But what I got from all this was; new contacts, new relations were developed, we saw their textile mills, their scale, and their style of working, saw their effluent treatment plants and our horizons widened. We got a completely new exposure and experience.

Consolidation & Expansion:

Due to my involvement in all these activities, my national connection started building up with Textile Ministry people. I was sought by other companies for solutions, even by our competitors. And we generously shared our knowledge with them.

People think that by sharing knowledge with our competitors, they will go ahead of us. But one must not forget that adaptability is a huge thing; we are ready to share but the receiver must also be open-minded enough to take in such lessons. Even if you share your best of the knowledge and ideas with them, the understanding, adaptability, acceptance and execution of their team might not be as intense as yours.

At that point of my life, I realized that we should never chase money, chase knowledge and money will follow you. Who was I to advice others, but I was. This happened due to my knowledge and research.

You need knowledge and a vision to break the traditional barriers set by the industry. I don't know why, but we all are strangely trained to chase money since our childhood, yet we never get it. I have practically earned through my knowledge.

In first half of 90's, we started learning on how to stabilize people and how to effectively delegate. Our business was small, single unit, yet we delegated the management responsibilities to properly selected professionals.

We are the only mill, which has people recruited in 1992 and are still there at leadership position. Whereas the local practice is that people switch jobs in couple of years.

> **❝** *In 1983, I got an opportunity to learn photographic printing technology at Switzerland. No one knew about it; it took 15 years for that technology to come to India. I was ahead of the rest.* **❞**

I always used to instruct them that, if I have to come inside the mill to solve any of the problems, you would have to leave your job and go out.

In 1995, I started working for garment fabric for export supply, while others were operating purely on job work, sourced from local market.

An exporter approached us with a specific requirement and there was no one who knew about those requirements. Because I was experimenting since 1992 and had made certain blunders, I knew about it. We started working with that exporter as a processing partner and till date our processing unit is 100% working only for export fabric for garment industry.

We were processing as per German standards and Germany was very strict on environment. If they find your fabric not matching with their requirements and standard, they will destroy the consignment and bill you for disposal. This expertise attracted C & A, Wal-Mart and many others, the whole Europe market was ready for us. We are the only registered company from Surat on the website of C&A for textile products.

With passing years, the same buyers demanded for eco-friendly dyes, fabrics etc. But we were flexible and fast to learn about these requirements and adapt to it.

In 1983, I got an opportunity to learn photographic printing technology at Switzerland. No one knew about it; it took 15 years for that technology to come to India. I was ahead of the rest. Learning takes you ahead of time.

At later stage in life, I did something, which was unthinkable for me till that time. I got a patent on my name. Actually I modified the Loopager, color fixation machine design for which I got a patent. It all happened because of all the learning's on environment studies and waste reduction techniques.

I can't put doctorate against my name because I don't have a formal degree in Engineering. I am a Diploma holder. I also did Diploma in Management in mid-90's.

> **❝** *One of my mentors, Mr. Kamal Tulsiyan asked me; if project fails, what would you lose? And will that loss force you to change your lifestyle? I said 'NO'. He said then go ahead and try it* **❞**

For my development, I was awarded by National Research Development Body in 2001 & by Govt. of Gujarat as a young scientist, in 2004.

Dr. Carve had interviewed me at the time of patent filing; he is an expert in Nuclear Science and Plasma. He was part of the jury and I was very much afraid. But if your content is right, nothing goes wrong.

I got the patent but I never wanted to commercialize this invention, so we shared it with the industry. Today approx. 200 companies are using this technology by modifying their machine. We are happy for this development.

I was socially very active with MANTRA, SGCCI, Trade associations and CII, environment division.

There was an issue and I represented the Association along with SGCCI. 35 companies were given a closer notice on environmental breach. I knew something so they took me to the court. I talked for 30 mins. in high court. No one is permitted to do that, but I was allowed. The closer was lifted in 3 days.

Knowledge always help, it helps you in networking. After this case, there are some six lawyers with whom I have got good relations even today.

My key driver is my passion for the subject. Textile is my passion and my first love. Environment came later as a hobby and became a passion too.

One fine day, one of my govt. friend asked me about why I don't take these environmental solutions as a business. This question struck me and I started thinking seriously about this. I also took advice from my mentors, father and friends. They encouraged me.

One of my mentors, Mr. Kamal Tulsiyan asked me; if project fails, what would you lose? And will that loss force you to change your lifestyle? I said 'NO'. He said then go ahead and try it. Mr. Arun Jariwala was also one such mentor who guided me in this issue.

> **Today, everyone has money and power. How will you differentiate yourself from them? Knowledge is going to be the only differentiator.**

My casual involvement with environmental issues led me to a new business opportunity and in the year 2000 our company GEPIL [Gujarat Enviro Protection and Infra. Ltd] came up with its first unit at Gabheni, Surat. We started with only landfill process.

Prior to that, in 1999, I went to Japan for 3 weeks training on this subject. In 2004, I went to Switzerland for 3 weeks training on hazardous waste.

All these opportunities come in your way, if you are willing to grab it. At the age of 40, you are actually going for classroom trainings, was not a comfortable thought for many. But this is how you differentiate yourself from others.

Today, everyone has money and power. How will you differentiate yourself from them? Knowledge is going to be the only differentiator.

First mover advantages are great, but first mover challenges also are difficult to handle. You make enemies just because you have grown.

Because of jealousy or some mistakes from few of our people, we faced a severe political challenge. There were lot of dharnas and negative publicity by print media and we were blamed with several allegations. Most of them were just rumors.

I challenge you to go out in market and check, whether anybody has not got their money back or if we have deducted any amount in the name of losses incurred. In-fact, we sold lot of our properties to manage the heavy losses that we had to incur due to this challenge.

Our balance sheets were constantly negative for 5 long years. At the beginning of this controversy, we had 100 cr. annual revenue and were planning to reach 500 crore. But due to this challenge, the revenues dropped to 50 cr. and now at present after all this struggle, we are somewhere at 100 crore revenues.

But whether we have good times or bad, we have not duped anybody till date and we will never do that ever.

> **“My prime purpose in life is to enjoy life and be happy always.”**

Little bit of Self Publicity is must:

I was an NCC Governor's medal winner for leadership. I have learnt that talent is not hideable, if you are producing results and performing, you will be recognized, sooner or later.

But later on in life, I have also realized that "Thoda self-marketing karna padta hai". If I had been good at marketing, I must have prevented the propaganda with counter strategy.

I am happy that my son Dhruv joined this company in turbulent times, have seen all these crises and have also seen us coming out of it and stabilize the business. I am sure he has got the learning of the lifetime and also about the harsh realities of business. So I can proudly say that at least my son is not the product of that over protected environment. Now he is tougher, we lost whatever we had to; but I still look at it as a positive thing.

Our happiness Index is high:

My prime purpose in life is to enjoy life and be happy always. Not only me, even after 5 years of bad patch, you look at my team, they are as happy as I am. Their Happiness Index is high. And that is why they have survived.

I wonder why 'Smart City' projects are not talking about Happiness Index of its citizens, why it is talking only about infrastructure? Why don't we ask, what will make our citizens happy? Let the city be happy.

Surti people are happy with small things. They are happy with Pokh or Ghari. (Locally popular sweet of Surat). Even if they own a Mercedes, they sit on footpath and eat, and enjoy a lot.

Current status:

Today Luthra group [GEPIL] has 12 operating plants across the country and are expanding further. In environment solution industry, we are one of the largest companies in terms of knowledge and infrastructure.

> **While shifting from family managed company to professionally managed company, the biggest challenge is at personal front, "Pehle toh hum khud hi nahi sudhrenge."**

I have been part of planning commission and involved in development of 12th five-year plan.

I also am engaged with Textile Ministry on developing Textile Policy and was being a part of environment policy making in early 2000. All this networking and knowledge helps a lot in your own business.

Modernizing the Business:

We in a very early stage realized that we can't grow in the textile business with traditional management style and structure and we need to bring in professional management system within the company. But for that, the first and foremost challenge was to professionalize ourself. We can't hire professionals or they won't stay with us if we are not professional and organized.

While shifting from family managed company to professionally managed company, the biggest challenge is at personal front, *"Pehle toh hum khud hi nahi sudhrenge."* (We ourselves will never improve).

But we took this challenge. We started hiring and developing the team of professionals. We also hired few senior retired professionals from some bigger organizations like Birla. This combination of senior and juniors has worked very well for us. There was some young professionals who were mentored by seniors and today they are the directors in the company.

We hired HR expert, Mr. Muthuswamy from Chennai, on retainer basis. We met accidently. He conducted an aptitude test of my son, which I liked, and then he did mine. I thought that this man is so good at understanding humans and if we have him with us, he will be an asset in our HRM and future leadership development process. Thus I asked him to conduct the aptitude test of my team.

He stayed with us for 10 years and did counseling. We learnt a lot from him on HR management. Even today, he is doing aptitude test of

> *Today I have such strong management and team that if you give me 24 hours and ask me to go out for 15 days, I will be ready. And in those 15 days, I will hardly receive 15 calls.*

new people. In our company, no senior appointment is done without the aptitude test. It happens online.

We constantly search for good people everywhere. The person we hired from Birla, he is our mentor even today and visits us thrice a week.

Our HRM practices are effective:

Innovation is also imp. for entrepreneurs to grow in any business. We have innovated a lot in our HRM Processes. We have created an index alongside the job description document, which had four criteria's, to which we have added new one.

For any position there are five major aspects apart from their JD.

E – entrepreneurial skills

I – innovation skills

M – managerial skill

S – supervisory skills

W – worker skills

Our aptitude test gives us a fair idea on this.

For lower rung jobs, we don't want entrepreneurial or innovation skills. But if we were hiring someone at the senior position, these two would have maximum focus. This tool helps us to select the right person for right job.

We have more than 250 people who are older than 25 years in this company. While longevity is good, it also has its own challenge. The seniors start taking you for granted. But when they see young professionals come in and go ahead, the problem is addressed.

> **For me life is about six things: Family, Finance, Health, Social, Mental and Spirituality (not bhakti). I try to balance all of them and believe in always being happy,**

My top management team members (CEO's and Directors) are under 45, majorly under 40. We have 10 CA's, 50+ Mechanical Engineers, and Junior Engineers & Doctorate holders too. Hiring and sustaining team of such caliber is critical. To sustain them and give them opportunity to innovate takes time and we need to give that time.

I am an SUV lover because it is safe. I prefer it even for my team. If they can't afford one, we will compensate the remaining amount but they should buy an SUV, if they are travelling for more than four days a month on highways.

People look at all this as an expense, which is a mistake. These are investments that produce excellent results in longer run.

Today I have such strong management and team that if you give me 24 hours and ask me to go out for 15 days, I will be ready. And in those 15 days, I will hardly receive 15 calls.

Balanced life is Important:

My first motto in life is to be happy: thus, I have lot of hobbies.

I am a professional photographer, a skydiver, a pilot and a leadership coach.

If I go to a wedding, I go there with my full kit, I go there and shoot, come back, develop the albums and gift it. Family feels good and is happy with this.

For me life is about six things: Family, Finance, Health, Social, Mental and Spirituality (not bhakti). I try to balance all of them and believe in always being happy, regardless of my external environment.

I travel 15 to 20 days a month out of which, business travel is just 40% and rest is social and trade development.

All these Chamber of Commerce, CII and Planning Commission meetings are great learning experiences. But for all this, the health must support. Thus, balanced life is important.

> *We are now basically an environment and industrial infrastructure company and are developing lot many industrial clusters.*

I am hungry to learn new things:

By being, a faculty or guest lecturer, I learn a lot. I have been to IIM Ahmedabad and Kolkata, they ask me such questions that forces me to think differently. I learn a lot from it.

Planning commission people think I am contributing, I think you have contributed to me. Primarily learning should be continuous. If I don't learn something new, I am in trouble.

From the humble beginning of 36 weaving looms to a national presence company, having 12 sites is a major achievement.

Our journey so far has been very exciting and wonderful. Till date we operated with Navision but now we are operating with ERP.

What is technology? It is knowledge about doing things differently with different processes. I read Business Maharaja's, written by Gita Piramal. I read the story of both; Reliance and Birla and I observed one thing. Birla believed, don't invest in technology, if it doesn't save money. Reliance said invest in technology, it will definitely save money. And who has grown faster today?

All locations for GEPIL are in multiple states with 30 to 40 crore investments at each of these sites. To manage this all, is not possible without right technology and management systems.

It also requires knowledge about several things, which I must have not got if I had sat in my office like other baniya mindset business owners.

People know me as I am today, but they don't know what I have done in past. I must have done more than dozen foreign tours just for the sake of learning, and all these tours were at the cost of my running business. I have been part of Indo-EU working group, Indo-Israel working group that was working on water technology project.

People these days say, Business is not working. To them I say, crying and cribbing is not an answer to challenges. Searching for an alternative business is also a project and requires meaningful involvement from you.

> *The problem is that people think of today or in terms of months, I think in terms of decades. So a bad patch for couple of years does not disturb me.*

There is an opportunity in every adversity:

During our turbulent time in past few years, I reduced my involvement in Chamber of Commerce, local trade bodies and trade association. But I increased my role in CII and other national bodies.

I have been a founder member for CII's newly developed unit for MSME. So if people say my four years were bad, no, it actually allowed me to do some new things. In fact, those were very good years for me.

GETP – Gujarat Eco Textile Park, our textile park was the first in India, after textile ministry came up with such plans and schemes. Till date it is one of the best. It is spread in 115 acres of land and one of the most beautiful industrial park you will see. After that, we did couple of more textile park projects in partnership with other companies.

We are also developing one more park exclusively for weavers.

Currently we are focusing on water waste and water recycle management services too.

We are now basically an environment and industrial infrastructure company and are developing lot many industrial clusters.

We have created GRAMZ [Gepil recycling and management zones] this is basically an eco-town which converts tons of waste into grams of waste.

For further scaling of this, we have, in collaboration with a Japanese knowledge partner signed and MOU with Gujarat govt. under Vibrant Gujarat. We have taken a mission that by 2021, Gujarat should be a landfill free state.

We also are the environment solution provider for DMIC [Delhi – Mumbai industrial corridor] and for that we have setup an infrastructure at Dahej, Gujarat. And are also setting up several hubs on the proposed corridor.

Our current employee strength is 1700 to 1800 people.

> **❝** *Good times stays for 5 to 6 years stretch and so is the bad patch. It is just up and down* **❞**

We are targeting 500 crore annual revenues by 2020 and we might go international with all our services in future.

Our social contributions:

Normally the success of an enterprise is measured through its financial balance sheet, but our success is measured through 'Green Balance Sheet'. Which reflects how much waste have we managed and helped for environment protection.

Our genes originate from the creed that says, 'We Commit'. And what do we commit? We commit green homes, green city, green state, green nation and a greener world.

We conduct cancer detection camps in rural areas and we run mobile dispensary, the needy in this country is everywhere.

I am proud of all my plant teams, because they are actualizing the ideology of this organization. They do all these social contributions in their respective territory and surrounding areas. They help the communities in which they operate, without my involvement.

Don't allow problems to block your growth:

Good times stays for 5 to 6 years stretch and so is the bad patch. It is just up and down. I had to drop Rs. 200 to 300 crore worth projects during my bad patch but does my life ends over there? No. We did not even downsize in that time, we kept full team intact.

If few years were bad, the next couple of decades are going to be awesome.

The problem is that people think of today or in terms of months, I think in terms of decades. So a bad patch for couple of years does not disturb me.

I once met with one of the Swiss bank professional. I asked him why people trust you so much. He said we bank for & with generations and not with any individual.

My Role Models Are :

1. Jamshedji Tata, he dreamt and created an enterprise in that turbulent time when britishers were ruling us. I wonder how he did this. It was really great
2. Warren Buffet, because of his simple philosophy of life. I will have what is needed and leave the rest. He has made lot of money but never wasted it and have been very simple during his entire life.
3. Dhirubhai Ambani, he taught Indians to dream big.

My advice to other entrepreneurs is:

- Keep a balance in life and give priority to all the important aspects.
- Keep innovation in mind and for that constant learning is must. Don't work to show to others, work for personal satisfaction and making meaningful contribution.
- Manage your time well – if your work does not complete on time, re-organize yourself. Don't ever say, that I am busy and over occupied
- Don't buy and wear brands to show it off to others, if this does not stop in Surat. It will become Delhi. [Today Mumbai has a many national level entrepreneurs, Delhi has few – because they are behind showing off]
- Educate yourself. For youngsters who think why study if we have to join the family business? You are wrong and this thought is misleading. Harvard survey reveals that 54% business fail in the hands of 2nd generation; only 7% business survives till 3rd generations.

REDEFINING THE INDIAN BEAUTY

Mr. Sunil Jain

Chairman

Firm Name:

Indian Women

Estd: 1988

Products & Services

Sarees & Fashion Apparels

Mr. Sunil Jain always dreamt about a life of achievement and prosperity and it was simply his perseverance that helped him realize this dream and made him the claimant to an over 100 crores INR turnover saree brand, 'INDIAN WOMEN' despite his humble roots. His enterprising nature and keenness to keep up with the changing times, have been the major contributor to his success.

Indian Women Fashion

"We don't chase sales target because I don't want to exist only for doing business and be busy in rat race. I want to live".

……. Sunil Jain

Mr. Sunil Jain, one of the founder and partner of Bahubali sarees and current owner of very popular saree brand 'Indian Women' narrates the story about journey so far.

I belonged to a lower middle class family and my childhood has passed with scarcity at Morena, MP.

There was a big haveli in our neighborhood and out of 365 days they used to have guests for almost 300 days. They had festival type environment in their house and most of the time there was a feast. Since their children were my friends, for playing I used to go to their house and always used to admire their lifestyle and prosperity. Since that time I used to dream about becoming like them. I always wanted to be a big man.

My first taste of Business:

My childhood friends were naughty thus education I received was average.

We had a retail shop of fabric and garments at a good location in Morena. At the tender age of 17, I requested my elder brother to allow

> **"Jitney log chhod ke jayenge, utna hi hamari pehchan badi hogi."**

me to travel to Mumbai along with him for purchase. That is when for the first time, I went out on a tour. During that visit I got lot of new ideas and exposure. Once I returned, I made some low cost modification in the display and layout. Because of these changes, we did very good business.

That exposure and experience boosted my confidence and self-belief. That is the time when I realized that I would do well in business.

I always used to experiment in my shop with new ideas. As part of that process, we changed the name of our retail store and the new name was "Ek Boliya", which means "One Rate". It was a kind of declaration that henceforth there won't be any bargaining in our store.

We strictly stuck to that image. Everyone knew that we are fixed rate store and we don't bargain. Because of that, we were very famous and became the landmark of the town. If you are new to the town and ask a rickshawala about ek boliya store, they will drop you at our place. We were that famous.

But to create and sustain such brand image, one also has to sacrifice a lot and suffer little pain. The habit of customers was such that they will always try to give lesser money. i.e. if the bill amount is 10111/- they will give us 10,000 or will try to reduce at least 11 rupees. But my nature was such that even if customer tried to give 1 rupee lesser than the actual bill value, I would not accept and thus lot of people used to leave the purchased material and go, out of their EGO.

We all used to feel bad about it. My brother used to get disturbed about it. But I always told him that, let them go, to build a brand, you need to take some risk. *Jitney log chhod ke jayenge, utna hi hamari pehchan badi hogi.* [More the number of people leave the store without buying; the stronger would be our image]

I was very hungry for growth and thus during that same period we tried lot of other businesses like trading in fertilizers (even today I don't know the difference between the color of fertilizers and ammonium

> ❝ My friends in my town encouraged me to come back to Surat and they said, whatever you do, you can't fail. You have good business sense. ❞

sulphide), pesticides, plotting, supplied political campaign material to MP congress committee members. Such gambles paid in long run.

We were doing business of 45 lakhs per annum by 1989 and that was a good turnover for the small town like morena. But I was not satisfied. I realized that if I want to be a big man, this shop in the small town won't be enough. I need to do something big and different

Journey to Surat:

I frequently used to visit Surat for purchase and used to stay near Bombay market. At night, I used to listen to the sound produced by the shuttle looms, it was a very sweet sound for me. It used to excite me and force me to shift at Surat.

Finally, I decided to shift to Surat and start some business over here. To prepare myself, I met lot of people and took suggestions and advice.

One well-wisher told me that: "if you remove one year in Surat without making any losses, you are good. If you can remove the interest of applied capital, you are an artist. But if you make profits, you are a smart businessman"

After this I went and met Sanjaybhai Sarawagi from laxmipati. He encouraged me and said, don't worry and go ahead.

We finalized a shop at rohit ac market, Surat in 1994 and decided to start the business of saree trading. But before we could distribute the invitation cards, flood and plague epidemic spread in Surat. So we went back to Morena.

My friends in my town encouraged me to come back to Surat and they said, whatever you do, you can't fail. You have good business sense.

So we came back. But one very good thing happened in this process, we left the Rohit market shop and decided to shift to Ashoka tower. The plan for rohit market was to produce low quality-low rate products but

> **Our entire production to delivery time was just 25 to 30 days against the industry practice of 60 to 75 days.**

ashoka tower was about better quality products. To produce better quality products required little more funds and risk, but we took a leap of faith. Mr. Harish from Parag sarees guided us and gave us the necessary support and encouragement.

In spite of fund crunch, we opted for better quality production and that was crucial decision. To manage the funds, we developed a partnership with Mr. Lalchand Baraiya, who is the current owner of our old brand 'Bahubali'.

What made us successful?

We always have tried to be different from other people of this industry. The market trend at that time was of six color matching but we started four color matching and that picked up.

Within six months we were profitable. It reminded me the statement of a well-wisher who had said that if; in one year you make some profits, you are a smart businessman. And here we had achieved that within six months. This increased our confidence and made us believe that we can do good business and we have good business sense.

One more step was to focus on reducing production cycle time so that we can do business with lesser capital. Our entire production to delivery time was just 25 to 30 days against the industry practice of 60 to 75 days. We also used to collect fast payments from the market so that our major business runs on our supplier's credit.

By this way we could maintain a healthy capital turnover ratio and reduce our production cost. This again helped us to sell our products at lower rates.

In those days the market system was working on 18% discount and thus the credit period was also long. We did not had money to give long credits so we decided to go on just 3% structure. As a result, our products

> **If the demand was of 1 lakh meter, we would produce only 50,000 meters and give short supply to all. As a result, there was a craving for our products in market**

were cheaper than the entire market. People purchased a lot from us and also gave speedy payments.

Within short period, market realized that the 3% discount system is better and thus all started following us. We were the trendsetters.

One important learning from that period was; never rely on any friend or well-wishers. Because; when you expect them to accept your terms and support you professionally, they say *"aap toh apne aadmi ho, aap to hume zyada support karoge"* which was not possible for us.

My retail experience was very handy in terms of dealing with customers and market presentation, Thus, we became a well-known brand in just 2 years.

One of the important strategy we implemented during that period was, we always maintained short supply of our products. If the demand was of 1 lakh meter, we would produce only 50,000 meters and give short supply to all. As a result, there was a craving for our products in market and people were desperate to buy from us. If you over supply, you will get sales but branding will never happen.

In those days when our dealers used to ask for 50 parcels, we used to supply them only 10 and remaining orders of 40 parcels were reserved for next few months. Thus, we always had advance orders for our sales. Hence, we did not had to worry about sales, all we had to concentrate was on new design creations, production and quality.

Constantly Evolved:

We kept on changing our product basket as per the need of the market. When there was a growing demand of stiff fabric, we launched stiff saree range. Dealers from the entire Indian market started working with us and that gave us good growth for next 3 years.

Business Stories

> *'Indian Women' has been a huge success, and within short span of 5 years it has crossed sales of Rs. 100 crores. This is a rare achievement for Surat market*

Once that dried out, around 1998, there was a trend for viscose based products, as an alternative to Banarasi sarees. we encashed on this trend too.

When this trend got dried, the trend of embroidery picked up. We created embroidery work based sarees, and to differentiate ourselves from others, we started embroidery work on printed sarees. Whereas the entire market was producing only dyed sarees with embroidery work. The idea worked and we got good response.

Once embroidery became a common thing, 5 years back, I realized that to create a different image we need to get into catalogue range of products, thus we launched a new brand 'INDIAN WOMEN' in year 2010.

Our existing brand 'Bahubali' was famous for different kind of product and qualities and we wanted to differentiate this product range from others. The product and price range for 'INDIAN WOMEN' was above Rs. 800 to 2000, but recently we also have added range of Rs. 700 to 800. These are wholesale rates.

'Indian Women' has been a huge success, and within short span of 5 years it has crossed sales of Rs. 100 crores. This is a rare achievement for Surat market; hardly few people could do this in such a short time in the entire history of Surat saree industry. It took 'Bahubali' 22 years to achieve sales of 100 crores.

To differentiate ourselves, we prefer to create designs with our own mind. We never follow our competitors or their product designs. We don't study other company's product and catalogues, this can be risky; if you focus on their products and design, you become like them and lose your originality and differentiation.

People often complain about mandi [recession] to which my response is very clear. If you have something different and new to offer, there is

> **Our strategy has been pretty simple. Average taste, reasonable rates and great quality**

no recession for you. But if you don't have anything different to offer, recession will definitely impact you.

Another important aspect has been our pricing strategy. Whatever products we create, our pricing strategy is such that even if somebody tried to copy our product, they can't sell it at our rates. Our rates are such that it is not an affordable option for our competitors to copy us. Our margin structure is very smartly planned.

Transparency is in our DNA. We are as transparent as glass. We have same price for all dealers, if retailer comes directly to us, he will get the rates at which our wholesale dealers sell them. Reason, we wanted them to buy from dealers and not from us.

We are non-compromising on policies and each person associated with us knows that. We have one common and clear policy for all, no duality in anything. At times people feel bad about this, but when they realize that our policies are common for all, they accept it.

Next big area of differentiation is quality control. Our product is checked at 5 stages before it reaches to the customers. We don't allow any defective product in market. As a result, our dealers and retailers know that product will not return from market due to quality related issues.

We believe that if some of our designs are not popular, it is ok, but if we supply 30 sarees to market, all 30 must sell due to its quality. Also our size cut is such that in the saree of 5.5 meters, our 90% sarees will be of 5.6 meters or 5.7 meters but won't be less than 5.5 ever.

In June 2015, we had a split in the company. BAHUBALI brand is currently owned by shri. lalchand baraiya, who was my business partner from last 22 years and INDIAN WOMEN brand is with us.

Due to the efforts of all these years, today, wherever there is a sale of saree, our products are available and the spread is so good that we don't

> **Paise ka koi moh nahi hai. Paisa bahot kamana chahta hu par uske liye raato ki neend kharab nahi karna chahta hu.**

have over dependency on any one state for our sales. Thus, any disturbance in particular state does not impact are sales adversely.

Just as dosa is popular and accepted as a common dish across India, Indian women should also be equally acceptable everywhere. We don't produce for any particular state or regional taste.

Our strategy has been pretty simple. Average taste, reasonable rates and great quality.

We have never chased revenue targets or sales – but have chased quality and better products. That is why our dealers have huge faith in us and even today we have advance pending orders. When the advance orders are in good numbers, then and only then, we marginally increase our production quantity.

At present we have around 100 people in our team.

Future:

In near future, we are planning to do something that no one ever has done. If it succeeds, we will be a different company altogether.

We don't chase sales target because I don't want to live only for doing business and be busy in rat race, I want to live.

Few years back, I realized this and discussed with my partner that we will operate only between morning 10 to eve. 8 and informed to all the stakeholders about this and immediately started the implementation.

At that point of time this was, and even today, this is unthinkable for the market. Because; the entire textile market and we too, used to operate till 9.30 or 10 pm. Majority of the traders still operate as per these timings.

This was exactly the timeframe in which embroidery trend had started. The production process and the production cycle time had increased

> **" I am detached with most of the things. Neither profit, nor loss disturbs me beyond a point. I forget it in hours. "**

on each saree. Turnover grew, workload grew, customers grew and we reduced working hours. People thought, it is madness and not practical.

But we did it and everyone; including our team and their families benefitted from this. I started leaving at 6.30 and my partner used to stay for little longer as he used to come little late in morning.

If you have proper planning and if your management is good, it is possible.

For our future, we are focusing on online sales and promotion. My son who has recently completed his CA is working on this project. We might also be launching salwar suits in near future.

Team contribution has been excellent

My role and involvement has decreased in day-to-day routine tasks and my team's role has increased. These days I just finalize products and do some follow up in critical aspects of production; the team does rest all the work.

Processing, packaging, sales, dispatch, accounts, collection etc. everything is done by the team. And they are doing it wonderfully.

I am peaceful person by nature and like to do business with peace. I never shout on my people. I believe, if you are good leader, they would be good. If you are peaceful, they will also be peaceful. All depends on us.

"Paise ka koi moh nahi hai. Paisa bahot kamana chahta hu par uske liye raato ki neend kharab nahi karna chahta hu". [I want to earn lot of money, but I am not a greedy person. I will never sacrifice my sleep and peace for the sake of money]

I want to fully enjoy my business. Whatever turnover we achieve is immaterial.

I am detached with most of the things. Neither profit, nor loss disturbs me beyond a point. I forget it in hours. This is the state for which people go to ashrams and Himalayas. I do business with great relaxation.

> **"** We can't contribute as an individual as much as what we can contribute as an entrepreneur through our business. **"**

Social Dreams:

I belong to Jaiswal Jain Samaj and want to create awareness in our community for entrepreneurship and encourage people to create bigger and better businesses. I also want to do something for the upgradation of the textile trade.

I had been the Member of FOSTTA, and consistently for three years I was in the managing committee. Last year I tried to develop a business forum of progressive minded people from textile industry. I also had conceptualized and launched a newsletter "Textile Samachar" on behalf of FOSTA, which reached to the circulation of 25,000, but later on the federation did not sustain it.

Why Business:

If you ask me; why I do business? I would say, Business is our identity, it creates employment, and it produces revenues for govt. through taxes.

We can't contribute as an individual as much as what we can contribute as an entrepreneur through our business.

Family support has been great:

I would say that behind every successful enterprise and entrepreneur, there would be solid support of family. Family support increases your belief, confidence and concentration. And that leads you to success.

My Family had been a wonderful support throughout this journey. My brother was elder to me but he supported me, trusted me and allowed me lot of freedom to experiment a lot in business.

Wife has always been on my side in all; good and bad times. Daughter was involved in my business till the time of her marriage and son is presently involved into the business and is my big support. Esp. after the partnership was dissolved.

> **❝** *My father asked me* "tu naukri karega ya aur logo ko naukri dega" **❞**

In our community, daughters are not encouraged much in business, but my daughter joined office for 2 years and she had done a wonderful job.

Constant learning has helped me a lot:

My learning history is very strong. I used to read lot of Hindi novels that helped me in developing my language command. It also had lot of hidden learning's, which I derived from them.

If your mind is open and if you are a genuine learner, you learn from everywhere and every day.

I am always attracted to education and studies. I was a dropout from 11th standard and wanted to complete my studies, thus, gave exam of 12th and then gave my B.com exams with just 7 days of studies.

Later I came to know that 7th Day Adventist College of Management had launched an executive MBA program. I enrolled myself in that program and was the eldest in that batch, but after 1 year of studies, right after my 2nd term exams I quit the course, mainly due to trouble with English language.

Because of constant learning I always feel that I am very young mentally and as energetic as any youngster

I learnt a very important lesson from my father, in my youthful days.

I had applied for a job and received an interview call but my father did not inform me about it. After the interview dates passed away, he shared the information with me and asked me *"tu naukri karega ya aur logo ko naukri dega"* This desire of him and his words also infected me and inspired me to become an entrepreneur.

In my retail days I was travelling a lot and have travelled almost half of India, and during that journey I had interacted a lot with different people and developed lot of insights and knowledge which has helped me immensely in my business journey.

I have learnt lot of good values from my parents and one of them is to serve others.

My role models are my parents and Mr. Harish Bhimani from Parag sarees. I have learnt a lot from him and got lot of encouragement and inspiration.

Advice for young aspiring entrepreneurs:

- Whatever you do, go deeper. Do with lot of commitment, focus and concentration.
- The youth thinks that young age is for enjoyment, but they forget that this is also the age of learning. Once you miss this age, you will regret for your whole life. My son at times compares with his friends who are roaming out while he is in office, I always tell him, they are roaming now and will struggle later. But you are learning business today and would be able to roam and enjoy for your entire life.

MEDICINE FOR GOOD BUSINESS

zota® healthcare ltd.

Mr. Kamlesh Zota

Director

Firm Name:

Zota Healthcare Pvt. Ltd.

Products or Services

Healthcare Products

From a small retail drugstore into a pharmaceutical giant that has nearly 100 crores INR turnover annually, Zota has been a story of gradual growth. Zota family has spurred such progress by relying on upgraded marketing strategies, persistent scaling of the business and widening the product basket. It's a story of how a small retailer can scale and create a successful company, if they have passion to grow and dreams to fulfill.

Zota Healthcare Pvt. Ltd

"We firmly believe in our ideological values and principles and never compromise on any of them. Some of the key values are; never compromise in quality and ensure best possible satisfaction with our service."

……… *Kamlesh Zota*

From a retail, medical store, started by Mr. Mukti Zota in Dhanera, Basantkantha district of Gujarat, Zota Pharma today stands tall in the pharmaceutical industry. Mr. Kamlesh Zota, Mukti's nephew recounts the journey.

After I joined my uncle's retail drug store venture, we started the wholesale business and recorded substantial profits. As the business started getting bigger and better and the customer base got broader, my uncle realized that the market salutes the seller.

There are lot many companies that manufacture medicines and OTC products but not all are good at marketing and sales. There were many struggling companies that had good products in their kitty but they could not sell. Since we knew the market trends well and knew how to sell, we decided to delve into creating our own brand of products with product outsourcing from existing drug manufacturers.

The venture under Zota brand started with initial five products in 1995. Protein syrup, iron syrup, paracetamol, folic acid and ranitidine tablets.

> **Our strategy has been; mostly, to acquire the existing companies with good products through takeover route.**

Current status:

Today we have, approximately 650 products and 2800 brands. Each drug is sold with separate brand identity and at times, also under multiple brand names. All the products are outsourced.

We do have our own manufacturing unit where we produce only for exports.

We have crossed Rs.85 crores last financial year and hope to be above Rs.120 crore this year. We have about 350 MR's and the network of 1250 distributors in as many as 30 states of India.

We are growing at 30% to 35% CAGR each year and looking at the market potential, we might continue with the same growth rate in coming years.

Drug research is one of our key focus area. We have six patented products out of which three have been commercialized. We have also filed patents for 11 more products.

Uptill now, we were into all prescription drugs, but soon we also would launch OTC products.

We have succeeded because we constantly study the market trends and requirements and keep on adding more products.

Our strategy has been; mostly, to acquire the existing companies with good products through takeover route.

Currently the business is being managed effectively within the family itself by nine of our family members, belonging to 2 generations.

Each has separate functional responsibility and are accountable for it. They are free to take decisions for their respective units. We avoid giving unnecessary advice and ideas to one another. Suggestions are given only when asked or if some confusion occurs.

Each has a clear role to play and a clear department to manage; Ketan Zota takes care of procurement of products. Kamlesh Zota of the legal, technical

> **We don't consider the routine issues as challenge. Routine issues are not problems, rather they are learning opportunities.**

and exports. Himanshu Zota takes care of accounts & marketing. Manu Zota of finance. Ashok Zota takes care of accounts along with Himanshu. Viren Zota, Niral Zota and Jatin Zota takes care of sales management and regional marketing of all the 23 division of drugs. And Moksesh Zota is in charge of the international marketing.

We are into exports from last four years and approximately 5% of our revenue comes from this. We have started supplying drugs to 10 countries from the African, CIS, South East Asia and Latin America regions.

Our Principles and policies:

Our organization believes in fair business and follows a policy of no business without bill. Hence, we don't supply any drugs through dubious deals or without proper bill. That is completely against our principle.

Maintaining exclusivity of distributors in allocated territory is our priority. We maintain exclusivity of all our distributors and no drugs are supplied to anyone, apart from our distributors in an allotted territory

Key challenges:

One of the major and a constant challenge that we face in this industry is government policies related to drug manufacturing and trading in India.

The next problem affecting us is manpower or getting the right people in the team.

Apart from these two, we haven't faced much of a challenge so far.

We don't consider the routine issues as challenge. Routine issues are not problems, rather they are learning opportunities.

> **Our Vision is to achieve a Global presence and a position among the top 50 drug companies of India.**

Teamwork works:

We have an excellent team and our teamwork has been commendable so far. In our case we just provide plans and leave it up to the team to execute. So far they have never disappointed us.

For human resource management, we focus on two simple basic points; first, we provide regular trainings to our people on products and other skills and second, we focus on the activities that increase their loyalty.

Future:

Our future is crystal clear to all of us because we all have together developed the future road map.

Our Vision is to achieve a Global presence and a position among the top 50 drug companies of India.

To us money does not matter that much and hence we never set any target for revenues or turnover.

In the future, we plan to enter the generic drug retailing business through JV with a multinational partner. Whenever launched, it would be technology enabled and a unique concept for the market and will benefit the customers in a huge way.

Very soon we are launching 'Nutravedic' an online retailing platform for nutrition products and the OTC drugs.

Key success factors:

Our success has been mainly due to quality, innovation and evolving as per market trends.

Since this is the knowledge economy and each business or any other organization operates with the help of the latest and updated knowledge, we too are very keen on learning.

> **We constantly keep an eye on competitors, understand their strategies and try to be better than them in all aspects.**

We all are qualified in pharmacy and use internet regularly for updating and above all, we have a very keen eye on studying the market trends closely.

We listen keenly to our sales team because they are the ones who meet the customers, the doctors and the distributors regularly.

We constantly keep an eye on competitors, understand their strategies and try to be better than them in all aspects.

Many of the family businesses have problems with internal management. Most of them struggle with the governance but this is not the case with us. We have a very strong unity amongst ourselves. We try and understand the nature and the priorities of each individual member of the family and have mutual respect.

Good governance structure, procedures and proper division of labor is also one of the reason why all nine of us are operating smoothly in our prescribed responsibilities.

We all meet daily for one hour and take status updates. The main purpose of these meetings is regular communication and performance analysis.

Our major focus has been on two aspects; one is to take over existing businesses with good products and potential & another has been market research.

Latest technology has empowered us:

Use of the latest technology again has been an important factor in our progress. Managing 650 products, 2800 brands, 350 MR's, operations and supply to 30 states. Ensuring right inventory at right time and at the right place is quite a challenging task. These challenges are intensified when the majority of your products are outsourced.

> **❝ The capital cost of software or technology might be high but the returns are great. ❞**

Technology is used in all the important aspects of our business. In marketing and promotion, in operations management, in inventory control (2800 SKU's), in data base management, in production, in quality control, in maintaining standardization and for knowledge upgradation. We all are dependent on technology.

Technology has helped us in many ways and especially for lean and profitable operations. With the help of technology, we could reduce the dependency on manpower, as there is an acute shortage of skilled manpower.

Despite outsourcing from several regions of the country, our overall inventory is under 45 days, which saves us a lot of capital and keeps our funds free for other important priorities. Our operational expenses are low which gives us competitive advantage in market.

The capital cost of software or technology might be high but the returns are great.

Family & society matters a lot:

Our family's constant support has been very useful. We worked till late nights in the initial business building years, we would go for lot of tours and even worked on Sundays. But they have remained patient with us and have provided the right space to us so that we are able to operate freely.

On the social side we are very active in our own capacity. We provide free of cost medicine to the needy, donate regularly for panjrapole [gaushala] activities, donate for community activities and events, provide medicine at a token cost for the community members.

Our advice to other entrepreneurs and youngsters is:

- Never compromise on your education, even if you have no intentions to get a job, or even if you have a ready family business to join. Get degree in suitable field. If you don't have the degree at present, learn and avail. But Don't just rely on degree, practical experience is must. Try to learn from other sources apart from academic books. Life has its own way to teach.
- Get proper knowledge and experience before jumping into any business. Avoid quick buck mindset, we might be doing 85cr business today, but it did not happen overnight. We might have spent sleepless nights for years before getting this success
- Go with the technology and market awareness

Final Note

Hope you have enjoyed reading these stories. Hope that each story has added some value to your knowledge base and have given you valuable insights on business.

Remember that;

"Encouraging The MSME Entrepreneurs and Youths To Create Big and Sustainable Businesses & Generate Employment Through Their Work Is The Core Objective Of Writing This Book"

If this book has inspired you to think big, do more and take more risks in business, then our objective is achieved.

Thank you for reading this book and respecting our efforts.

See you soon with next edition from different city of India

Aslam

www.ingramcontent.com/pod-product-compliance
Lightning Source LLC
Chambersburg PA
CBHW031614210526
45464CB00004B/1566